VICTORIA'S
FINAL DECADE

1890s

VICTORIA'S FINAL DECADE

1890s

Jeremy Harwood

 Reader's Digest | gettyimages

CONTENTS

1890s IMAGE GALLERY
FRONT COVER: A crowd of parents and pupils from Charterhouse School attend a special Charterhouse Matinee at the Haymarket Theatre, London, in 1899.
BACK COVER: One of the official photographs of Queen Victoria taken for the Diamond Jubilee in 1897, to commemorate her 60 years on the throne.
TITLE PAGE: A group of young boys, some of them barefoot, enjoy having their picture taken sitting on the edge of the fountain outside the Walker Art Gallery, Liverpool, in about 1895.
OPPOSITE: Hay-making involved a lot of labour-intensive work by hand, and family, friends and visitors were usually roped in to help. This photograph of people with hand-rakes was taken in summer 1895.
FOLLOWING PAGES:
Taking samples from barrels on West India Quay, London docks, in 1893.
Firemen on duty by their fire engine in the City of London in the aftermath of the Bread Street Fire, 1899.
A holiday crowd, complete with Easter bonnets, dancing to a tune played on harmonica on Hampstead Heath, north London, during the Easter Bank Holiday break in 1892.
An audience of mixed ages enjoys an open-air concert on the beach at Yarmouth in 1890.

THE **NAUGHTY** NINETIES

For the rich and well connected – the people who could afford to dine at London's Cafe Royale, or pop over to the Moulin Rouge in Paris to see Louise Weber dance the can-can – the final decade of the 19th century was dominated by the pursuit of pleasure. Most folk lived more hard-working, humdrum lives, but all shared a pride in their country, its vast empire and the seemingly immortal Queen Victoria. Her days of unpopularity were long gone and she was revered throughout the land, her name adorning streets, railway stations and institutions of every kind. As her Diamond Jubilee approached, it felt as though she had ruled for ever. For most of her subjects, she was the only sovereign they had ever known.

ROYAL FAVOURITE Lady Daisy Brooke, who became the Countess of Warwick when her husband inherited the title. One of the great beauties of the late Victorian age, she was a social icon and the Prince of Wales's mistress for nine years.

A BAD CASE OF FLU

It was a new and momentous decade, but it started cold, miserable and wet. In Findon, a sleepy Sussex village with a population of around 770, the rain was so torrential some of the cesspools flooded, setting a river of raw sewage flowing along the High Street. A vile stench pervaded the village – even the wind, it seemed, could not blow it away – and the smell lingered long after the sewage had finally disappeared.

This was not the only problem faced by Findon's inhabitants. In the winter of 1890–91, in common with the rest of the country, they were hit by an influenza epidemic. The local school closed as all of the teachers took to their beds. Most of the pupils were suffering from the illness as well. The initial outbreak did not appear too serious, but a second epidemic began in April 1891 and went on until early June. In Sheffield, it raged through the city; Bradford and Huddersfield were just as badly affected. At the peak of the outbreak, more than 100 people were dying each week. Epidemics kept recurring: the southeast of the country suffered just as badly the following year and the Midlands was hit the year after that.

Doctors were powerless. They did not know what influenza was, or have any effective means to treat it. In desperation, people turned to Turkish baths, carbolic vaporisers, medicinal wines and anti-bacterial lozenges, hoping to hold the disease at bay or at least to relieve some of the symptoms.

Wet, wet, wet

Winter ended, but the bad weather continued. That summer, farmers complained of a ruined harvest, while in Manchester, for the first time in cricket history, incessant rain forced a Test match between England and the touring Australians

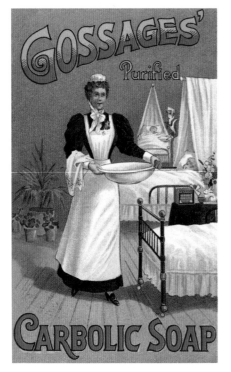

HOSPITAL CARE
Nurses and patients in a typical cottage hospital ward in Ireland. Health conditions were slowly improving, but doctors had little to offer sufferers during the influenza pandemic that struck in 1890. Known as 'Asiatic flu' because of its origins in Central Asia, the disease spread swiftly and its consequences were often fatal. Dr Bruce Law, a physician at St Thomas's Hospital in London, wrote the following notes: 'The invasion is sudden, the patients can generally tell the time when they developed the disease. This sudden onset is often accompanied by vertigo, nausea and sometimes actual vomiting of bilious matter. There are pains in the limbs and a general sense of aching all over, frontal headaches of special severity, a general feeling of misery and wretchedness and great depression of spirits.' Vigorous scrubbing with 'purified carbolic soap' helped to improve general hygiene in hospital wards, but could not check this disease.

QUACK CURES AND RECUPERATION

Influenza was extremely debilitating and was no respecter of class. Lord Salisbury, the Prime Minister, was ordered by his doctors to the South of France to convalesce after catching the illness. The *Star of Gwent*, a local newspaper in Wales, chronicled how influenza 'has pervaded the great majority of homes and it is feared that the death rate ... will be far above the average. The Mayor has been confined to his rooms, whilst many leading inhabitants suffering from colds and fearing an attack of influenza are deeming it prudent to remain within doors.' Peddlers of patent medicines were quick to take advantage of the public's fears. This advertisement for the Carbolic Smoke Ball appeared in the *Illustrated London News* in January 1892. The makers claimed almost miraculous powers for their product and confidently offered £100 to anyone who could prove they had contracted influenza despite using a smoke ball.

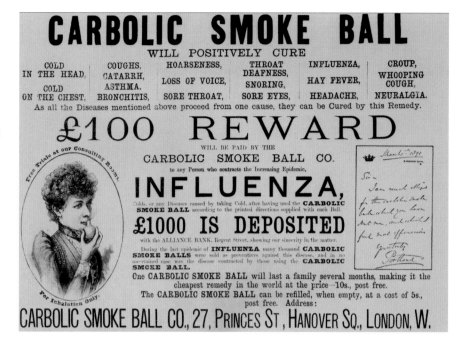

to be declared a draw without a ball being bowled. Fortunately, thanks largely to the redoubtable batting of Dr W G Grace, England were already two games up in the three-match Test series and so retained the Ashes. The victory gave bedraggled Britons something to celebrate.

BRIDGING THE FORTH

CRICKETING LEGEND

Dr W G Grace, the Gloucestershire and MCC all-rounder, was in his fourth decade of playing first-class cricket. Though no longer the lithe, athletic figure he had been in his youth, he was still breaking records. In May 1895 he became the first man ever to score 1,000 runs in a month. The Prince of Wales telegraphed his 'heartiest congratulations on a magnificent performance'. Over the course of a 46-year career, Grace scored 54,896 runs, including 126 centuries, and took 2,876 wickets. When he died, in 1915, the *Manchester Guardian* hailed him as 'by common consent the greatest and most attractive figure that has ever appeared on the cricket field. In his mastery of the game, in the length of years during which he stood above all rivals, in the amazing total of his cricketing achievements and by no means least of all in the popular interest he excited. No cricketer, living or dead, has yet approached him, and it is doubtful if any ever will.'

Another cause for cheering was the opening of the great railway bridge across the Firth of Forth on 4 March, 1890. The event drew crowds from all over Scotland, plus a whole posse of distinguished foreign visitors, including Gustave Eiffel, the man who had built the Eiffel Tower.

The Prince of Wales, who was to perform the opening ceremony, was not troubled by the bad weather on the long journey north. He travelled in a new saloon carriage specially built for the occasion by the Great Northern Railway. According to *The Scotsman*, it contained 'a luxurious sitting room, two bedrooms, a smoking room, lavatories, a servant's apartment and a kitchen with cooking apparatus ... the decorations and upholstery are upon the most elaborate scale and the saloon is without doubt one of the most comfortable and beautiful carriages that has ever run in this country'. The royal carriage was heated by hot water and lit by electricity. For the Prince the most essential feature may well have been the smoking room. His usual practice was to smoke two Egyptian cigarettes and a vast cigar by the time he sat down to breakfast. His smoking continued throughout the day, amounting to another 20 cigarettes and 12 giant cigars by dinner time.

On arrival in Edinburgh – his train came in early – the Prince was greeted by the Lord Provost, local magistrates and members of the City Council before

continued on page 22

THE FORTH BRIDGE

Spanning the mighty Firth of Forth to provide a direct railway link between Edinburgh and the north of Scotland, the great Forth Bridge was officially opened in 1890. As part of the opening ceremony, the Prince of Wales tapped in the last rivet (below), which was gold plated to mark the occasion.

The Forth Bridge was the first major bridge in the world to be built of steel – 54,000 tons of it were used in the construction, along with nearly 7 million rivets. The design was the work of engineers John Fowler and Benjamin Baker, who settled on a cantilever construction to take the place of a suspension bridge, plans for which were hastily abandoned after the Tay Bridge disaster of 1879. It took from 1883 to 1887 to erect the three giant cantilevers supported on granite-faced piers (above and above right), then another three years to link them together with girder spars secured to the structure by huge pins. The completed bridge has an overall length of more than 1½ miles. Baker, who was knighted by the Prince for his achievement, commented: 'If I had pretended that the building of the Forth Bridge was not a source of constant anxiety, present and future, no experienced engineer would have believed me.'

leaving for Dalmeny, where he was to be the guest of Lord Rosebery, his host for the occasion. Characteristically, Rosebery was late. The bridge, which the Prince had already visited during its construction, was officially opened the following day.

It certainly was a masterpiece of Victorian engineering. Jointly designed by engineers John Fowler and Benjamin Baker, it had taken up to 5,000 men, working day and night, seven years to build. At least 57 workmen were killed in accidents while the bridge was being constructed; eight others were saved from drowning by the safety boats stationed on the river below. From start to finish, the massive project cost £3,250,000 (in today's money, more than £230 million).

Because of a strong wind that had blown up – one observer noted that the weather 'grew more boisterous and disagreeable, the wind being accompanied by heavy showers of rain' – the actual opening ceremony was somewhat truncated. All that the Prince managed to say to the crowd of onlookers was 'Ladies and Gentlemen, I declare the Forth Bridge open'. He was rather more fulsome at the banquet that followed, before returning to Dalmeny where he later boarded the royal train for the journey south back to the capital.

IRISH IMBROGLIO
Irish-born Sir Charles Russell (top), an ardent supporter of Home Rule, was one of the most prominent lawyers of the day. He represented Charles Stewart Parnell before a judicial commission set up by the government to investigate charges against the Irish Nationalist leader that had been published in *The Times*. Russell utterly demolished the case against his client. Journalist turned Liberal politician John Morley (above) was another staunch Home Ruler who acted as Gladstone's chief negotiator with the Irish Nationalists. Tim Healy, a leading Nationalist, joked that if the Liberal leader was the 'Grand Old Man', Morley was the 'Grand Old Maid'.

A BLOW TO IRISH HOME RULE

Lord Rosebery, who had been the Prince's host in Scotland, was a leading figure in the Liberal Party. Many spoke of him as the most likely successor to Gladstone, when the Grand Old Man finally decided to retire. The acerbic Beatrice Potter – soon to become Beatrice Webb on marrying Sidney Webb, another leading light of the recently founded Fabian Society – wrote off Gladstone as 'senile'. She was just as scathing about other leading members of the Liberal shadow cabinet: John Morley was 'a moral preacher', Sir William Harcourt 'a windbag and weathercock'. Rosebery, she concluded, was 'the best of the lot'.

But the Liberal leader had no thought of retirement. On the contrary, Gladstone was convinced that it would not be long before he was in office again as Prime Minister; he believed that God was preserving him for that very purpose. Though his party had split asunder over Home Rule for Ireland, Gladstone had remained remarkably sanguine, even after a landslide defeat by the Conservatives and their Liberal Unionist allies in the 1886 general election. Now, as he jocularly told a London audience, he seemed to be 'popping up again' everywhere.

By-elections told their own story: the government lost contest after contest. By 1890, the Liberal Party managers were predicting a majority of around 100 seats in the next election. A sweeping victory would give Gladstone the mandate he needed to press forward once more with a Home Rule Bill. He told Dr Ignaz von Dollinger, a German theologian he had known since 1845, that unless he himself were to die or Charles Stuart Parnell, the leader of the Irish Nationalist Party, were to be removed, the success of the Home Rule cause seemed assured.

Gladstone was fortified in this belief by what had happened after *The Times* published a series of articles accusing Parnell of conniving in the Phoenix Park murders. The case against the Irish leader collapsed when the letters on which *The Times* had relied as evidence were demonstrated to be fakes. Richard Pigott, the journalist who had forged them, broke down under cross-examination by Sir Charles Russell, Parnell's barrister, and promptly fled the country leaving a confession behind him. Pigott was eventually tracked down to a hotel room in Madrid, where he shot himself dead as the Spanish police, armed with a warrant for his arrest, burst through the door.

The fact that Lord Salisbury and other members of the Cabinet had supported *The Times* in what turned out to be baseless charges only added to the government's unpopularity. Parnell became a public hero practically overnight.

Parnell – from hero to villain

When Parnell entered the House of Commons for the first time after his vindication, he received a standing ovation from the packed Opposition benches. Even the Liberal Unionists – with the notable exception of Lord Hartington – and a few Conservatives joined in, while Gladstone rose and bowed deeply to the Irish leader. He set the seal on Parnell's public rehabilitation by inviting him to stay at Hawarden Castle, his country home in Wales, at the end of the year.

It was Parnell's great moment of triumph. It was to be short-lived. Seemingly out of nowhere, a scandal broke that turned public opinion completely on its head. It also shattered the alliance – the so-called 'Union of Hearts' – between the Liberals and the Irish Nationalists, on which all Gladstone's hopes for Home Rule were based. It had long been known behind the scenes that Parnell was having an affair with Catherine O'Shea, wife of Captain William O'Shea, the Nationalist MP for Galway. O'Shea had known of his wife's adultery for years, but kept quiet about it in the hope that it might help him achieve a position of power. He was also paid by his wife to keep silent. Now, with his hopes of office disappointed, O'Shea filed for divorce citing Parnell as co-respondent.

The Irish leader seemed to take the news calmly. He assured an anxious John Morley, the shadow Chief Secretary for Ireland and Gladstone's personal emissary, that he would triumph as overwhelmingly in the divorce court as he had done before the government's judicial commission. He took the same line with Michael Davitt, one of his most prominent Irish Nationalist supporters. Gladstone, Parnell's parliamentary followers and, even more crucially, the Catholic Church in Ireland all took him at his word.

The case went to court in November 1890. There, to everyone's astonishment, Mrs O'Shea openly admitted adultery. Neither she nor Parnell proffered any defence. O'Shea was granted a *decree nisi* and a storm then descended on the Irish leader's head. Lord Salisbury commented contentedly that 'the scandal has brought out an uprising in favour of domestic purity which we must all regard with the deepest satisfaction'. *The Times* savoured its revenge: 'Domestic treachery, systematic and long-continued deception, the whole squalid apparatus of letters written with the intention of misleading, houses taken under false names, disguises and aliases, secret visits and sudden flights make up a story of dull and ignoble infidelity untouched, as far as can be seen, by a single ray of sentiment, a single flash of passion, and comparable only to the dreary monotony of French middle-class vice, over which the scalpel of M Zola so lovingly lingers.'

The pressure on the Liberal leadership rapidly mounted. Letters and telegrams poured into Hawarden, demanding that Gladstone break off contact with the Irish

ILL-FATED LOVERS
Charles Parnell's undoing was his love for Kitty O'Shea, his mistress of many years, pictured above in a photograph taken in about 1880. Her husband, the Irish Nationalist MP Capt William O'Shea, had condoned the liaison for years, but on Christmas Eve 1889 he sued for divorce, naming Parnell (below) as the other party. Parnell assured both Irish Nationalists and Liberals that he would emerge from court without a stain on his character, but he underestimated the stigma of infidelity and divorce. His fall from power was swift. The Liberals turned against him, his party split into two warring factions and the cause of Home Rule was fatally undermined.

SOCIALIST BELIEVERS
Beatrice and Sidney Webb were the leading lights of the Fabian Society, which had been founded in 1884. Both were passionate believers in the need for radical social reform. Sidney became Professor of Public Administration at the London School of Economics, which he and his wife founded in 1895, and played a central role in the formation of the Labour Party. Beatrice was just as intellectual and influential. She started out as a social researcher, working with her cousin Charles Booth on his report into conditions among the poor of London's East End. She became a socialist, she wrote, 'not because I believe it would ameliorate the conditions of the masses (though I think it would do so), but because I believe that only by communal ownership of the means of production can you arrive at the most perfect form of individual development, at the greatest stimulus of individual effort'.

Nationalists. Sir William Harcourt, reporting back to his leader after a meeting of the National Liberal Federation in Sheffield, told Gladstone bluntly that the Nonconformists, the backbone of the party, were in revolt. The Catholic Church was equally adamant. Cardinal Manning urged the hapless Gladstone to denounce Parnell publicly and called on the Irish bishops to do the same.

The only thing, it seemed, that could save Parnell was for him to renounce the leadership of the Irish Nationalist Party. From South Africa, the multi-millionaire magnate Cecil Rhodes cabled his succinct advice: 'Resign – marry – return!' But the beleaguered Parnell had no intention of resigning, even temporarily. Gladstone accordingly wrote him a letter in which he stated that Parnell's 'continuance at the present moment in the leadership would be productive of consequences disastrous in the highest degree to the cause of Ireland'. He gave the letter to John Morley with instructions to track Parnell down and make sure he read it before the Nationalist MPs met to elect a leader for the next session of Parliament.

Parnell, though, was adept at covering his tracks and avoided meeting Morley until after he had been re-elected at the party meeting. When Morley finally managed to find him, Parnell dismissed the outcry against him as a 'storm in a teacup'. Under no circumstances would he resign. As soon as Gladstone heard the news, he ordered his letter to be published.

Nationalist MPs were confronted with the starkest of choices. They could give in to Gladstone and abandon their much-loved leader. Or they could continue to follow Parnell and run the risk of sacrificing the chance of Home Rule. Almost inevitably, they failed to do either. After 12 days of acrimonious debate in a House of Commons Committee Room, the party split into two warring factions. The larger group – 44 MPs strong – followed Justin McCarthy into secession. The remaining 26 stuck by Parnell, who continued battling. Almost immediately after the crucial vote, he hurried across to Ireland to campaign for a Parnellite candidate

CATHOLIC PILGRIMS
An open-air Mass at the Shrine of Our Lady in Knock, County Clare, where thousands of sick pilgrims congregated to pray to be cured. Though himself a Protestant, Parnell had won over the bulk of Irish Catholics to the Home Rule cause. But after the O'Shea divorce case the Church hierarchy turned against him. Cardinal Manning told the Irish bishops that 'plain and prompt speech was safest'. They responded immediately. The Archbishop of Dublin urged the Nationalists to depose their leader, while a sermon condemning his immorality was ordered to be read in the pulpits of every church in the land. The *New York Times* reported that Parnell's hopes had vanished.

LOVED BY THE POOR

One of the greatest religious leaders of the age, Cardinal Manning started his career as a High Church Anglican parson before converting to Roman Catholicism and being ordained as a priest. His funeral in 1892 was one of the biggest London had ever seen. After a requiem mass conducted by 16 bishops at the Brompton Oratory, priests and monks were joined on foot by trade union representatives and many others in the funeral procession to Kensal Green cemetery. Thousands turned out to pay their respects as the Cardinal's coffin passed by; at some points along the route the crowds were so dense the procession was forced to a halt. After playing a crucial part in helping to settle the Great London Dock Strike of 1889, Cardinal Manning said of his conversion: 'If I had not become Catholic, I could not have worked for the people of England, as in the last year they think I have worked for them.'

at the Kilkenny by-election. It was to no avail. The Catholic Church spoke out against him: 'You cannot remain a Parnellite and remain a Catholic,' one priest told his flock. Parnell's candidate was roundly beaten. Further humiliations followed in North Sligo and Carlow. The increasingly exhausted Parnell fought on until ill-health forced his return to Britain. He died in the arms of Catherine O'Shea in Brighton on 6 October, 1891. They had married that summer.

Ireland had lost the man who was probably the greatest leader it had ever produced. As for Gladstone, though he soldiered on, John Morley reported that he had never in his life seen the Grand Old Man so depressed.

SCANDALS IN HIGH SOCIETY

For months, the newspapers were full of little other than Charles Parnell and Catherine O'Shea, but two further scandals broke at around the same time, both involving people from the very highest ranks in the land. The first incident, after an initial flurry of interest, was successfully hushed up, but the second led to no less a personage than the Prince of Wales being forced to make a reluctant appearance as a witness in open court.

The first scandal began in October 1889, when the police raided what turned out to be a male brothel in Cleveland Street, off Tottenham Court Road, London. Various grandees were involved, including the Earl of Euston, son of the Duke of Grafton, and Lord Arthur Somerset, son of the Duke of Beaufort and equerry to the Duke of Clarence, the Prince of Wales's eldest son, and superintendent of the Prince's stables. Lord Arthur fled to France to avoid arrest; the Earl stayed to face the music, eventually successfully suing his accusers for libel.

A ministerial intervention?

The question was, who had tipped Lord Arthur off and so given him the time he needed to make his escape? Henry Labouchere, the left-wing Liberal MP for Northampton and owner of *Truth* magazine, was sure that he knew the answer. He believed that none other than the Prime Minister, Lord Salisbury himself, had warned Sir Dighton Probyn, the Prince of Wales's comptroller and treasurer, in a hurried meeting at King's Cross Station that Lord Arthur faced arrest for gross indecency. Probyn then told the unfortunate peer, who fled the country before the warrant for his arrest could be issued.

SCENTING SCANDAL
Radical Liberal MP and magazine owner Henry Labouchere (top right) was quick to scent Tory scandal when Lord Arthur Somerset – seen here (bottom right) in a caricature by Spy – was allowed time to flee the country rather than face arrest for gross indecency. Labouchere was hardly liberal when it came to homosexuality. He was author of the so-called 'Labouchere amendment' to the Criminal Law Amendment Act, which made any homosexual act between males a criminal offence. It was under the terms of this Act, as amended by Labouchere, that Oscar Wilde was later convicted.

On 28 February, 1890, in a 75-minute speech in the Commons, Labouchere accused the government of 'a criminal conspiracy' and Lord Salisbury of lying. This was too much for the Speaker, who suspended Labouchere from the House for a week. His motion demanding an enquiry into the allegations was defeated by 206 votes to 66. Salisbury was unperturbed. On 3 March, defending himself in the House of Lords, he said he had indeed met with Probyn 'for a casual interview for which I was in no way prepared, to which I did not attach the slightest importance, and of which I took no notes whatever'. The only thing he admitted was telling Probyn 'that rumours had reached me that further evidence had been obtained, but I did not know what its character was'. Concluding his statement with the remark that 'the subject is not one that lends itself to extensive treatment', he sat down contentedly to the cheers of his fellow peers.

If Salisbury did warn Probyn of the likelihood of Lord Arthur's arrest, he almost certainly acted out of a spirit of class solidarity with a fellow aristocrat and

SPORT OF KINGS AND PRINCES
The Prince of Wales loved racing, which replaced shooting as his favourite sport. He is pictured here with Richard Marsh, his trainer, and his 1896 Derby winner, Persimmon, with jockey John Watts in the saddle. Most people were delighted with the royal victory, though Lord Rosebery, whose horses had won in the previous two years, commented that everyone would say that the other runners allowed the Prince to triumph. The Prince's winnings on the turf were considerable – in 1896 and 1897 alone, he earned almost £44,000 in prize money – but so, too, was his expenditure, which usually exceeded his income.

to save the Duke of Clarence from possible embarrassment should the case come to court. The Prince of Wales was all for hushing the entire thing up. At first he simply refused to believe the accusations. Then he commented that Lord Arthur must be an 'unfortunate lunatic' and the less that was heard 'of such a filthy scandal the better'. He told the Prime Minister he was pleased that Lord Arthur had been allowed to flee; he further asked that if Lord Arthur should 'ever dare to show his face in England again', the authorities should allow him to visit his parents in the country 'without fear of being apprehended on this awful charge'.

A game too far

The second scandal was not dealt with quite so effectively – and this time, much to Queen Victoria's horror, the Prince of Wales was directly involved. It all began at Tranby Croft in Yorkshire, the country house of Arthur Wilson, a wealthy shipowner, where the Prince had gone to stay for the St Leger race week in Doncaster in September 1890. The story climaxed the following June with a trial in open court. It involved baccarat, a favourite card game of the Prince, which had recently been declared illegal.

Over two consecutive evenings Sir William Gordon-Cumming, a lieutenant-colonel in the Scots Guards, was separately observed by five other members of the

BACCARAT PARTY
The house party at Tranby Croft that led to the baccarat scandal. Sir William Gordon-Cumming, who was accused of cheating by his fellow house guests, is seated to the left of the Prince of Wales. The Prince, having warned his old friend that denial was useless, did his best to bury the affair, but it became public knowledge when Sir William sued his accusers for slander. The Prince was appalled to be summoned as a witness. Gordon-Cumming's conduct, he said, was 'simply scandalous' and his version of events 'false from beginning to end'. When the jury found against Sir William, the Prince wrote to his son, Prince George: 'Thank God! – the Army and Society are now well rid of such a damned blackguard.'

house party to be cheating at cards. What Sir William was doing, it was alleged, was using sleight-of-hand to manipulate his gaming counters after looking at his cards, an illicit manoeuvre that stacked the odds in his favour.

When confronted with the accusation, Sir William hotly denied the charge, but to no avail. He was told bluntly by Lord Coventry and Lieutenant-General Owen Williams, two of his fellow-guests, that unless he signed an agreement that he would never play cards again, public exposure would follow. The unhappy baronet protested that signing such a document would be tantamount to admitting his guilt, but eventually he agreed to do so. The Prince added his signature as a witness. In return, Sir William's accusers and the other members of the house party agreed to keep silent about what had transpired.

The secret gets out

All might have been well had the promised secrecy been preserved, but news of the accusation leaked. Afterwards, it was widely supposed that the Prince must have spoken of the affair to Lady Daisy Brooke, his favourite female companion at the time, and that she had been unable to keep the story to herself. Indeed, her addiction to gossip had earned her the nickname 'Babbling Brooke'. In any event, it was clear that someone had let the cat out of the bag. Sir William responded by ordering his solicitors to bring an action for slander against the five original accusers. He also instructed them to subpoena the Prince as a witness in court.

To be forced to appear in open court would be a serious embarrassment for the Prince, so he and his friends tried to thwart Sir William's action. First, they pressed Sir Redvers Buller, the adjutant-general, to set up a secret military court to inquire into the baronet's conduct. At first Sir Redvers agreed, but then changed his mind when he was told that such proceedings could be deemed unfair. The Prince trumpeted his displeasure to the Duke of Cambridge, the army's commander in chief. 'It is enough to make the great Duke of Wellington turn in his grave and point the finger of scorn at the Horse Guards', he complained. 'The conduct of the adjutant-general is inexplicable ... I always knew that he was a born soldier – and equally imagined he was a gentleman, but from henceforth I can never look upon him in the latter category.'

Next, they tried to get an inquiry set up by the Guard's Club, but the members voted it down. Sir Francis Knollys, the Prince's private secretary, explained the thinking behind the plan to Sir Henry Ponsonby, private secretary to the Queen. 'The great object is to put an end to the action ... and the best way to achieve that end would have been for the Guard's Club to have turned him [Sir William] out ... There would then, in all probability, have been an end of the whole affair, and people ... could have talked about the case being pre-judged as much as they liked.'

The Prince on trial

It seemed there was no alternative but to allow Sir William Gordon-Cumming his day in court. The case began before Lord Chief Justice Coleridge on 1 June, 1891. Sir Edward Clarke, the solicitor-general representing Sir William, did not spare the Prince's feelings. He claimed that the innocent baronet was being victimised to save the honour of the Prince, who was in the habit of encouraging the playing of an illegal game and who had mistakenly jumped to a wrong conclusion when presented with the flimsiest of evidence. Furthermore, he accused the Prince of

ENJOYING A GAME OF CARDS
Many Victorians saw nothing wrong with a quiet game of cards, provided that the stakes, if any, were minimal and the company respectable. Some games were more acceptable than others. Napoleon, usually shortened to Nap, was a family favourite. In *Three Men in a Boat*, J, the narrator, tells how he, George and Harris played penny Nap to while away a wet evening on the river: 'We played for about an hour and a half, by the end of which George had won four pence – George always is lucky at cards – and Harris and I had lost exactly two pence each. We thought we would give up gambling then. As Harris said, it breeds an unhealthy excitement when carried too far. George offered to go on and give us our revenge; but Harris and I decided not to battle any further against Fate.'

LEGAL EAGLES
Sir Edward Clarke (near right), solicitor-general in Lord Salisbury's administration, represented Sir William Gordon-Cumming in the Tranby Croft court case. Believing his client to be totally innocent, Clarke argued that Sir William was the victim of a conspiracy designed to cover up the Prince of Wales's involvement in the scandal. Sir Francis Knollys, the Prince's private secretary, complained to Lord Salisbury that the Cabinet 'ought to have taken steps to protect him [the Prince] from the public insults of one of the Law Officers of the Crown'. The Prince also protested that Lord Coleridge (far right), the judge who heard the case, did not intervene to put a stop to Clarke's attacks.

deliberately flouting War Office regulations, which laid down that, in any case of supposed dishonourable conduct, the entire matter must be submitted to the accused's commanding officer.

For the next few days, the Prince was a fixture in the courtroom. Many people across the land believed that, rather than the defendants, it was the Prince himself and his way of life that were on trial. When the time came for him to give evidence, he spoke in such a low voice that only a few of his answers could be heard. This, as the editor of the *Daily News* noted, created a bad impression in the crowded public gallery. When the jury finally brought in a verdict against Sir William, it was greeted by a protracted outbreak of angry hissing.

The Prince's popularity plummeted. He was booed loudly when he attended the races at Ascot and attacked vociferously in the press. *The Times* expressed its regret 'that the Prince should have been in any way mixed up, not only in the case, but in the social circumstances which prepared the way for it'. On the other side of the Atlantic, the *New York Times* advised its readers that 'the scandal cannot fail to add to the growing conviction that "royalty" is a burden to the British taxpayer,

'What does concern and indeed distress the public is the discovery that the Prince should have been at the baccarat table; that the game was apparently played to please him; that it was played with his own counters specially taken down for the purpose; that his "set" are a gambling, a baccarat-playing set.'

The Times, 1891

for which he fails to receive any equivalent'. Back home, the *Review of Reviews* was even blunter, stating that 'various country gentlemen', whom its editor had interviewed, thought that the Prince should be condemned as 'a wastrel and a whoremonger' as much as for being a gambler. It was not so much baccarat as 'the kind of life of which this was an illustration that was the cause of their disgust'.

Though sympathetic to her son's plight, the Queen understood the depth of public feeling. It was not just 'this special case – though his signing the paper was wrong (and turns out to have been contrary to military regulations)', she wrote to her eldest daughter, 'but the light which has been thrown on his habits which alarms and shocks people so much, for the example is so bad ... The monarchy is almost in danger if he is lowered and despised.'

The Prince paid careful heed to Lord Salisbury's advice, which was relayed to him via Lord Hartington. 'I should recommend him to sit still and avoid Baccarat for six months', the premier wrote, 'and, at the end of that time, write a letter to some indiscreet friend (who would publish it), saying that, at the time of the Cumming case, there had been a great deal of misunderstanding as to his views; but the circumstances of the case had so convinced him of the evil that was likely to be caused by that game, that, since that time, he had forbidden it to be played in his presence.' The Prince wisely decided to give up baccarat for bridge.

UNDERLYING TRENDS

What ordinary folk really felt about the goings-on in high society depended to a large extent on their circumstances in life. On the surface, or so it appeared, things were going well enough. South Wales, for instance, was rapidly becoming the fastest-growing industrial area in the kingdom through the development of its coal mines and the iron and steel industry. But the underlying trends in industry and agriculture were not so favourable: farming in particular was still mired in deep depression, while foreign competitors like the USA and Germany were making their presence felt in industry.

Even the City of London had its problems. In 1890 Baring Brothers, the oldest and, next to Rothschild's, most prestigious merchant bank of the day, came perilously close to crashing following ill-advised investments in South America, notably in Argentina, where the bank had incurred liabilities it could not repay. The ensuing panic was halted by the Bank of England, which moved swiftly to orchestrate a major rescue operation. Around £17 million was raised from other banks, including the Rothschilds, to save the struggling Barings.

Life of a nobody
Generally, lower middle class City clerks, like George and Weedon Grossmith's immortal Mr Pooter in *The Diary of a Nobody*, had never had it so good. Pooter's ramblings had originally appeared in *Punch*, but in the summer of 1892 they were published in book form and became an instant bestseller. For Mr Pooter and his ilk, life was, on the whole, easier than it had ever been. The family was

continued on page 42

VICTORIAN HOME STYLE

The Victorians spent a substantial amount of time and money turning their drawing rooms into a reflection of their position in society. This room (left) is in the so-called Aesthetic style that became popular in the 1890s. As well as the essential items of furniture, homemakers were advised to be on the lookout for ornaments – figurines, bronzes, lithographs and glass domes filled with curios – to add that final decorative touch. The flush lavatory was becoming commonplace in domestic homes, but this deluxe model, advertised in about 1890, was aimed at the richer end of the market.

The Osborne family from Northampton (below), pictured in their Sunday best in the back yard of their terraced home. Families like the Osbornes were the pillars of middle-class respectability – William Osborne (standing) was a well-known grocer in the town.

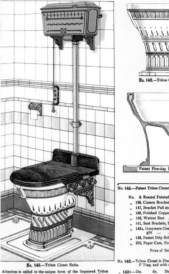

WORKING FOR A LIVING

No one was more class-conscious than the British. Awareness of class permeated all walks of life, and none more so than the world of work. In the mines, in the shipyards, on the factory floor, skilled workers guarded their rights and privileges against any attempt to upset the status quo. As the economic woes of the 1890s worsened, many employers attempted to force down wages, and the result was a series of strikes and lock-outs. Governments of both Liberals and Conservatives proved reluctant to intervene. Charlie Glyde, a noted trade union activist, summed up the position in 1891: 'We have had two parties in the past, the can'ts and the won'ts, and it is time we had a party that will.'

NEW AND OLD
Post Office workers load a wagon with mail for the new Imperial Penny Post service launched in 1898 (right). The innovation was pushed through Parliament by John Henniker Heaton, a Conservative backbencher. As a young man making his fortune in Australia, he had known what it was like to be too poor to write home.

Working for the Post Office was an eminently respectable job. It was safe, fairly well paid by the standards of the time and brought with it a smart uniform. The woman at the tiller of this barge on the Grand Union Canal had a less certain future. Bargemen and women did not have the best of reputations. Some of them swore or drank too much and, what was worse, worked on a Sunday. They were also part of a dying trade. The great days of the canals were over and the goods once carried by the barges were now largely transported by rail.

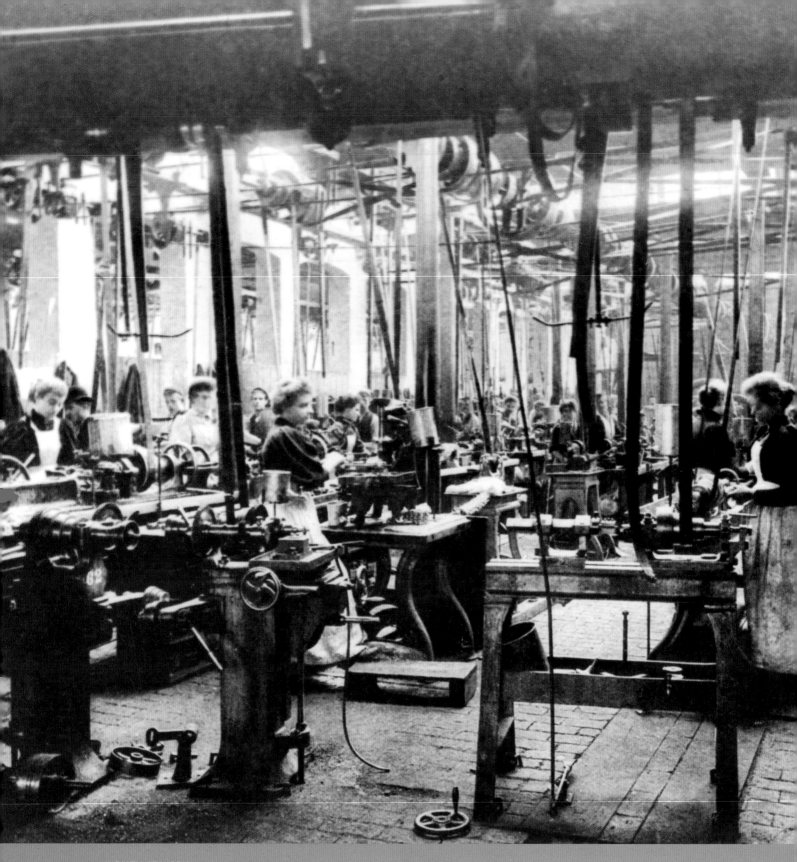

WOMEN AT WORK

For many Victorians in the 1890s, the notion of women working was still, quite simply, not acceptable. A woman's place, it was deemed, was in the home, looking after her husband – the breadwinner – and children. Nevertheless, women were taking up paid employment in increasing numbers. The jobs open to a woman very much depended on the social class to which she belonged. Factory machine-workers, like these women hard at work making bicycles in the Midlands, were working class.

Cycling was one of the success stories of the decade; at the height of its popularity, 750,000 bicycles were being made and sold each year. The belts coming down from the ceiling in the factory delivered power to the individual machines from a central engine.

One of the few professions open to middle-class women was nursing (top right). Another, increasingly since the building of Board Schools, was teaching. Many women took up a position as a governess, but this was often a sign of having fallen on hard times.

Older women often worked at home. These Northamptonshire lace-makers (right) are taking advantage of a fine day to take their work into the garden. For many, domestic service was the only option: in 1890, there were more than a million female servants across the country.

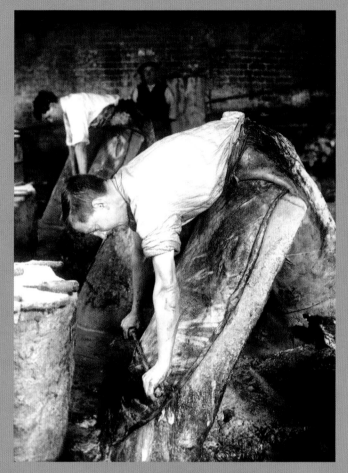

SKILLED AND UNSKILLED

Some jobs required special skills. Captain Massey Shaw, long-serving Chief of the Metropolitan Fire Brigade, insisted that all his firemen (far left) were former sailors. He believed that the training taught men discipline and made them hardy. They needed to be. Victorian firemen worked long hours, night and day, for low wages and they lived at their fire stations.

Leather tanning required few special skills (top left), but was physically demanding. These men are working on hides in a tannery in Bermondsey, a centre of the Victorian tanning and leather trades. Many preferred to set up by themselves as street traders. This Italian knife-grinder (left) is sharpening a knife on a portable grindstone, which he transports in his barrow along the streets of London.

NEW DIRECTIONS

The coming of the telephone was a catalyst for change in women's employment, as the telephone exchange quickly became a female domain. This operator is manning the Manchester exchange, which became operational in 1895. But it was the arrival of the typewriter that really sparked change, as women found the machines easier to operate than men. When the first wave of female typists – lady typewriters as they were originally known – hit the business world in the 1890s, the office changed to suit them. Rolltop desks, bottles of ink and scratchy pens were on the way out. It was a major step forward for women. Typing paid better than most other jobs and offered pleasanter working conditions. Soon, typists were rising to become stenographers and secretaries, both hitherto male preserves.

newly installed in a rented house in suburban Holloway, within striking distance of his work in the City. They could afford a maid, who doubled as cook, and a charwoman to help with the cleaning. 'The Laurels', their house in Brickfield Terrace, was typical of the times: 'a nice six-room residence, not counting basement, with a front breakfast parlour' and 'a nice little back garden which runs down to the railway'. This was the house's drawback. 'We were rather afraid of the noise of the trains', Pooter records, 'but the landlord said we should not notice them after a bit and took £2 off the rent.'

A wind of change

People like the Pooters were natural Conservatives, the products of what Lord Salisbury had called 'villa Toryism', which he had done much to foster through his cautious policy of social reform. The government had also succeeded in imposing peace on an unwilling Ireland. Arthur Balfour, the Chief Secretary and Salisbury's nephew, might have won himself the soubriquet 'Bloody Balfour' for the uncompromising coercive policies that he implemented, but alongside these he also introduced some much-needed land reforms. With Ireland apparently pacified, support for Home Rule outside that country dwindled – and so did Gladstone's hopes for a big parliamentary majority when the general election was called. Salisbury soldiered on as Prime Minister until almost the very end of Parliament's legal term, until finally deciding to go to the country in July 1892.

> 'The question of the unemployed is to me of such importance that I would be unfaithful and untrue to every election promise I made if I did not count on it receiving due consideration at the hands of any Government ...'
>
> **Kier Hardie, House of Commons, 1895**

At the age of 82, Gladstone embarked on his last election campaign. In truth, he was a shadow of his former self, his voice and energy fading as he harangued electors from the platform. His eyesight was failing, too, not helped by the fact that, while speaking at Chester, he had been struck in the eye by a hard piece of gingerbread thrown at him by a woman in the crowd. Small wonder that the Queen, whose Conservative sympathies had grown and grown, wrote that 'the idea of a deluded excited man of 82 trying to govern England and her vast Empire with the dismal democrats under him is quite ludicrous. It is like a bad joke.'

The election was close run. The final result gave the Liberals 273 seats. In addition they could count on the support of the 81 Irish Nationalists, plus the first-ever independent Labour MP, James Keir Hardie. This gave Gladstone a rag-bag majority of 45 seats over the Conservatives and the Liberal Unionists.

The election of Hardie, a former miner and Liberal turned socialist, was a herald of the future. He had stood for Parliament once before, when he came bottom of the poll. This time he contested the election in West Ham, in the heart of London's East End, as an Independent Labour candidate – and won the seat. He broke with all tradition by arriving at Parliament wearing a cloth cap and tweed suit, instead of the regulation top hat and frock coat. It was a clear sign that politics in Britain were beginning to change.

LABOUR PIONEER

The illegitimate son of a Lanarkshire farm servant, Keir Hardie began work as a baker's delivery boy when he was just eight years old. At the age of 11, unschooled and illiterate, he went down the pit and became a coalminer. By the age of 17, with some help from his mother, he had taught himself to read and write. He worked in the mines for 13 years, before starting his political rise as a trade union activist. In 1892, the year this picture was taken, he was invited to stand as an independent Labour candidate in West Ham in London. He won, and so became the first socialist MP in the Commons. The following year he was part of the group that formed the Independent Labour Party.

Hardie announced himself as a radical in Parliament right from the beginning. Scorning convention, he arrived at the House to swear the oath and take his seat for the first time wearing not the black frock coat and top hat favoured by conventional Conservative and Liberal politicians, but dressed in a tweed suit and cap. In policy he was equally radical, favouring woman's suffrage, higher taxation for the higher paid to fund free schooling and pensions for the working class, and self-rule for India. He came in for heavy criticism in the press following a speech attacking the privileges of the monarchy, a stand that may have contributed to him losing his seat in the 1895 election. He was re-elected, for Merthyr Tydfil, in 1900.

TOWARDS THE
END OF AN ERA

When Gladstone regained power in 1892, he had only one real political ambition remaining – to give Ireland Home Rule. In the event, his Home Rule Bill was thrown out by the House of Lords. Having quarrelled with most of his Cabinet colleagues – he described them variously as 'mad' or 'drunk' – Gladstone resigned for the last time in 1894. Lord Rosebery, the Foreign Secretary, took over as Prime Minister, but his leadership was weak and his administration hopelessly divided.

WASTED TALENT Gladstone was not the only one to have a disappointing end to his career. Oscar Wilde was cut off in his creative prime in 1895, when he was convicted of gross indecency and sentenced to two years' hard labour. He never recovered from his prison ordeal.

GLADSTONE'S LAST STAND

I t is said that all political careers end in failure, and Gladstone's return to power in 1892 was certainly an anticlimax. The general election had not produced the great Liberal majority he had been counting on to carry Irish Home Rule through Parliament. Instead, the results were curiously inconclusive.

The total poll rose from 2.75 million to 4.4 million, but by no means all of the newly enfranchised voters were Liberals. On the contrary, the Conservatives, counted with their Liberal Unionist allies, remained the largest single party in the House of Commons, with 313 seats against the Liberals' 272. Gladstone was forced to fall back on a coalition with the 81 Irish Nationalist MPs to give him a lead of 40 seats. Lord Salisbury derisively termed it a 'motley majority', but it was still enough to force Salisbury's resignation when the Conservative government failed to vote down a Liberal amendment to the Queen's speech. The speech was the shortest in living memory, amounting to no more than a few lines. The following day, the defeated premier made his way to Osborne House, the Queen's summer residence on the Isle of Wight, to proffer his resignation.

Gladstone forms his last government

The Queen took leave of Salisbury 'with regret', then reluctantly summoned Gladstone to take office. Her opinion of him had not improved. She confided to the Marquis of Lansdowne that she had no wish 'to entrust the Empire to the shaking hand of an old, wild, incomprehensible man of 82'. She was not encouraged when he arrived for his audience. She noted that Gladstone – or Merrypebble, as she had privately nicknamed him – was 'greatly altered and changed, not only much aged, walking rather bent with a stick, but altogether; his face shrunk, deadly pale, with a weird look in his eyes, a feeble expression about the mouth, and the voice altered'.

Gladstone's impression of the Queen was every bit as unfavourable. He told Sir Edward Hamilton, once his private secretary and now the rising star of the Treasury, that it seemed to him the Queen's intellect had become sluggish and her judgment impaired. To Sir Algernon West, who had volunteered to assist Gladstone after retiring from the Inland Revenue, he wryly commented that his interview with the Queen had been as dismal as if between Marie Antoinette and her executioner.

THE GRAND OLD MAN
Gladstone and his wife Catherine relaxing in the park at Hawarden Castle, their home in North Wales, accompanied by one of their grand-daughters, Dorothy Drew. Not long before, in the same park, Gladstone had narrowly avoided death when he was attacked and knocked to the ground by a wild heifer. He lay very still, pretending to be dead, until the animal was distracted. Then, bruised and shaken, he got up, dodged behind a tree and made his escape back to the house. After the heifer had been shot, an elaborate wreath arrived at the castle. The anonymous inscription on the accompanying card read: 'To the memory of the patriotic cow which sacrificed its life in an attempt to save Ireland from Home Rule.'

LIFE SAVERS – THE RNLI

By 1890, the Royal National Lifeboat Institution (RNLI) was well-established around Britain's coasts. That year, a steam-powered lifeboat was launched; the images here show more typical boats of the decade. All crew members – like these three men from North Deal (left), the crew of the Skegness lifeboat (right) and the full boat crew below – wore standard cork life-jackets, invented in 1854.

People all over the country were quick to recognise the bravery of the all-volunteer crews when the first national flag-day was held in 1891. The spur for the flag-day was the *Mexico* disaster. On a stormy night in December 1886, three lifeboats – from St Anne's, Lytham and Southport – responded to distress rockets fired by the German cargo vessel, which was in trouble off Southport. The St Anne's lifeboat vanished without trace. The Southport boat was swamped by a freak wave as it neared the *Mexico* and capsized. Only the Lytham boat made it back to shore. In all, 27 lifeboat men perished; the German crew was saved.

LIBERALS AT LOGGERHEADS

Sir William Harcourt (near right) and Lord Rosebery (far right), respectively the Chancellor of the Exchequer and Foreign Secretary in Gladstone's last government, were the two chief contenders for the premiership after the Grand Old Man retired. The pair disagreed over practically everything. They also disliked each other intensely and their relationship steadily deteriorated. Things got so bad after the Liberals were routed in the 1895 General Election that Rosebery decided 'not to meet Harcourt in council any more'. Harcourt, who was notorious for his bad temper, called Rosebery's attempt to exclude him 'a damned piece of impertinence'. Harcourt continued to lead the Liberals in opposition in the House of Commons, while Lord Kimberley led the few remaining Liberal peers in the House of Lords. The following year, Rosebery resigned the overall leadership of the shattered party. Harcourt became de facto leader until he, too, decided to retire in 1899.

Rosebery had won – as he did over a subsequent crisis in Egypt and another in Siam (Thailand) – but his victories had an adverse affect on his long-standing friendship with Gladstone. Relations between the Foreign Secretary and Prime Minister degenerated to freezing-point and never really recovered.

THE SECOND HOME RULE BILL

Apart from Home Rule, Gladstone had shown little interest in the proposals the Liberals put before the electorate in 1892. The cynics said that their Newcastle Programme – a rag-bag of radical measures that Gladstone reluctantly launched at a meeting of the National Liberal Federation in Newcastle in October 1891 – had been designed deliberately to appeal to as many pressure groups and competing factions as possible, both within and outside the party. Temperance campaigners, municipal progressives, Welsh devolutionists, House of Lords abolitionists, education reformers and proponents of Scottish and Welsh disestablishment of the Church were all among the campaigners now demanding that Gladstone's government give priority to their particular hobby horse.

The only one of the demands that Gladstone had some sympathy with was the call for change in the House of Lords. Observers of his Newcastle speech noted that while he was attacking the peers he raised his arms higher and higher, as though invoking the wrath of Heaven, while his knees sank lower and lower until it looked as if it must end with them touching the platform's bare boards. The rest of the Liberal programme he glossed over or simply ignored.

It was Home Rule that mattered – and that alone. Closeted with John Morley, his Chief Secretary for Ireland, Gladstone devoted himself personally to drafting and redrafting a new Home Rule Bill that he was determined should become law.

Most of his Cabinet colleagues knew little of the Bill's detail as late as three days before it was presented to the House of Commons on 14 February, 1893. What they did know was that Gladstone had originally called the measure a 'Bill for the Better Government of Ireland', but at the opening of Parliament a fortnight earlier Queen Victoria had flatly refused to include the words 'Better Government' in her speech. Gladstone was forced to re-title it a 'Bill to Amend the Provision for the Government of Ireland'. He introduced it with a characteristically marathon speech of his own lasting two-and-a-half hours.

The Conservatives and Liberal Unionists let the First Reading pass unopposed. Then they launched their attack. Arthur Balfour, the Conservative leader in the Commons, denounced it as an 'abortion of a measure'. That April, standing in for his ailing uncle Lord Salisbury, Balfour had visited Belfast to rally Ulster support for the Unionist cause. It did not take much rallying. His sister Alice, who was travelling with him, recorded: 'Every house was decorated with flags; every window was full of spectators, and the streets were packed with men, women and even children, so that it seemed carriages would never get through ... The pressure must have been terrific, shouts of men and screams of women coming up at every moment, till one became so possessed with fear that some horrible accident would take place that one could hardly give attention to the oncoming procession.' It took so long for the loyalists to march past the reviewing stand that a tall stool had to be provided for a tired Balfour to lean on.

Home Rule rejected

As the bitter parliamentary struggle continued tempers rose to fever pitch, especially when, in order to push the measure forward, Gladstone invoked a guillotine to cut short the debate. The tension climaxed on 27 July during a speech by Joseph Chamberlain, who had once been the rising star of the Liberal benches but was now leader of the Liberal Unionists and counted among the Conservatives. As he launched a virulent attack on the Prime Minister, he was interrupted by shrill cries of 'Judas!' from the Irish parliamentary benches. Within a minute, a near riot erupted on the floor of the House. Arthur Griffith-Boscawen, a newly elected Conservative MP and witness to the fracas, later recalled that the next morning the cleaners swept up 'a broken arm of a bench, some buttons, several shirt studs, and a false tooth'. The pugnacious Ulster Tory backbencher Colonel William Saunderson claimed that the fight started when he was struck on the head from behind by a Nationalist MP.

Despite the vehement opposition, Gladstone did manage to steer his Bill through the House of Commons. It passed its third and final reading there on 2 September. It then went to the House of Lords, where it was given short thrift. The Lords threw it out by a crushing 419 votes to 41 on 8 September. The rejection was moved by the Duke of Devonshire, as Lord Hartington had now become, and Lord Salisbury himself wound up the debate. 'If you allow this atrocious, this mean, this treacherous revolution to pass', he harangued his fellow peers, 'you will be untrue to the duty which has descended to you from a splendid ancestry; you will be untrue to your highest traditions; you will be untrue to the trust that has been bequeathed to you from the past; you will be untrue to the Empire of England.' The Conservative leader left the House in triumph, making his way through an enormous crowd that was busy letting off celebratory fireworks and singing 'Rule Britannia'.

'BLOODY BALFOUR'
Golf was a favourite pastime of the Conservative politician Arthur Balfour, shown here on the cover of *The Graphic* news magazine in May 1890. His aggressive style of play showed a ruthlessness that was fully revealed in his administration of Ireland. When Lord Salisbury, his uncle, appointed him Chief Secretary to Ireland in 1887, the Irish Nationalists, aware of Balfour's relative youth and inexperience, christened him 'pretty Fanny'. But his suppression of Irish unrest soon changed their opinion. They gave him the new nickname of 'Bloody Balfour' after he congratulated the police who had opened fire on an unarmed crowd at Michelstown. Needless to say, Balfour was utterly opposed to any notion of Home Rule. He promised the House of Commons that he would be 'as relentless as Cromwell in enforcing obedience to the law, but, at the same time, I shall be as radical as any reformer in redressing grievances'.

THE ORANGE HALL BELFAST. R.W.

MADE IN BELFAST

Belfast, the Ulster capital, was a Protestant stronghold. It produced great ships, fine linen and a host of other things, including well-known mineral waters. Bottled water was a flourishing industry in the Cromac district in the south of the city, where artesian wells supplied non-alkaline spring water. William Corry and Co's aerated waters – the company also produced lemonade and ginger ale – were 'prepared exclusively from the limpid waters of Corry and Co's celebrated Cromac spring'. The company's promotion claimed the waters were 'guaranteed free from metallic and other impurity' and 'recommended by the most eminent Analytic Chemists of the day'. South Belfast was also home to many of the city's wealthiest merchants and industrialists.

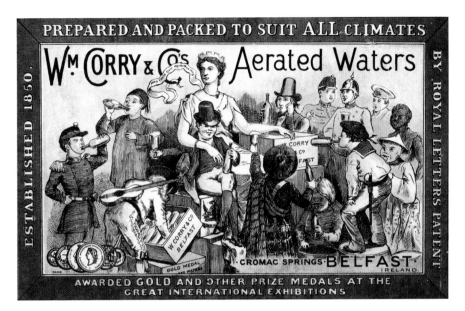

With the exception of Gladstone, his most loyal supporters and the Irish Nationalists, few were disappointed by the rejection of Home Rule or recognised it as an important opportunity lost. Nationwide, it seemed that most people were bored by the interminable controversy. Wiseacres joked that when the House of Lords threw out the Bill, not a dog barked from John O'Groats to Land's End. Secretly, even some of Gladstone's Cabinet colleagues were relieved that it seemed to be over. When he urged them to consent to the dissolution of Parliament and an appeal to the country to uphold the rights of the people who had elected him over the unelected peers, they simply refused to support him.

ORANGE STRENGTH

Protestant loyalists gather outside the Orange Hall in Belfast. The Union Jack and Ulster's own banner fly proudly from the roof. The date of 1690 on the building's frontage commemorates the year that William of Orange defeated James II at the battle of the Boyne, preventing the deposed Catholic king from staging a comeback to the English throne.

The Orange Order, which was founded in 1795, led the fight to preserve the Union with Britain. It was at one of the Order's meetings that Lord Randolph Churchill had coined the celebrated rallying cry 'Ulster will fight and Ulster will be right'. The wildly enthusiastic audience gave him a standing ovation. Arthur Balfour enjoyed a similar reception when he visited the city in 1893. He was guest of honour at a mammoth four-hour Orange march-past. Alice Balfour, who was with her brother on the reviewing stand, was astonished, she recorded, by the near-hysteria of the crowd.

ALL ALONE

Thwarted in his primary intention, the Prime Minister pressed ahead with a Bill to establish employers' liability for accidents in the work place and another increasing the powers of Parish Councils. If the peers tampered with such reforming legislation, Gladstone believed that the country would react in his favour after all. The policy – 'filling the cup' as it was termed at the time – was continued by Rosebery, who took over as Prime Minister when Gladstone finally resigned.

When Gladstone's resignation came, in March 1894, it was unexpected. Even after the defeat of his Home Rule Bill, he had seemed in no mood to consider retirement. Indeed, in a speech in Edinburgh he announced that he would be reintroducing much the same measure in the next session of Parliament. Then something happened that turned politics upside down. Gladstone had a major disagreement with colleagues about the estimates for the naval shipbuilding programme proposed by Lord Spencer, the First Lord of the Admiralty. In arguing that the estimates must be reduced, Gladstone found himself practically alone.

Ship design had improved so much in recent years that the existing British battle fleet was in danger of being outclassed by those of rival powers. Recognising this, the previous Conservative government had committed itself to the so-called

FULL REGALIA
Lord Spencer, Gladstone's First Lord of the Admiralty, warned the Cabinet in 1893 that the admirals believed France and Russia would both achieve numerical supremacy over the British fleet within three years unless a major new shipbuilding programme was undertaken. Spencer accordingly pressed for an increase in the naval spending estimates. He was opposed by Prime Minister Gladstone and by the Chancellor, Sir William Harcourt, who dismissed the calls for a bigger navy as alarmist. In a speech to the House of Commons in 1893, Harcourt was emphatic, insisting that there was 'one thing the government are not going to do. They are not going to propose to build a number of ships and leave their successors to pay for them.' But the rest of the Cabinet backed Spencer and eventually even Harcourt came round to his point of view. More ships would be built. It was the issue that drove Gladstone to resignation.

The naval construction programme proposed by Lord Spencer, First Lord of the Admiralty, called for the building of 10 battleships, 38 cruisers, 18 torpedo boats and four fast gunboats.

THE SURVIVOR

HMS *Camperdown* (below) was repaired following her disastrous collision with HMS *Victoria* in June 1893 during naval manoeuvres in the Mediterranean. Vice-Admiral Sir George Tryon was in overall command of the exercises, operating from the *Victoria*, flagship of the Navy's Mediterranean fleet. It was his confusing orders that led directly to the *Victoria* being rammed by the *Camperdown*. She sank in just 15 minutes, giving many of her crew little chance of survival: 358 men, half of the crew, perished. Tryon himself went down with the ship, reputedly murmuring 'It's all my fault'. The *Victoria*'s captain, Maurice Bourke, survived to face a court-martial. It ruled that Tryon alone was to blame. Bourke and Rear Admiral Sir Albert Markham, commander of the *Camperdown*, escaped with mild reprimands.

'two power standard', which pledged that the Royal Navy would be maintained at sufficient strength to deal with any two enemy fleets at the same time. Initially, the Liberals supported the naval construction programme, which called for the building of no fewer than 10 battleships, 38 cruisers, 18 torpedo boats and four fast gunboats. Now Gladstone had changed his mind and he accused Spencer of surrendering to what he termed 'a conspiracy' on the part of the Sea Lords. Spencer, supported by his colleagues, stood firm.

In early January 1894 Gladstone harangued the Cabinet without pause for nearly an hour on the folly of accepting the disputed estimates, but only George Shaw-Lefevre, the First Commissioner of Works, gave him any support. A naval disaster in the Mediterranean the previous June had already served to remind the others how narrow was the margin of safety on which the country was currently relying. During manoeuvres, HMS *Victoria* and HMS *Camperdown*, the two best British battleships of the day, had somehow managed to collide. The *Victoria* quickly sank and the *Camperdown* was seriously damaged. Sir George Tryon, the Admiral in command of the Mediterranean fleet, went down with his flagship.

continued on page 63

LIFE IN 'THE QUEEN'S NAVEE'

In 1878, the 'Queen's Navee' had been the setting for Gilbert and Sullivan's first big stage hit, *HMS Pinafore*, and as the Victorian Age neared its end, there was no doubt that life in the Navy was much more humane than it had been for previous generations. Instead of being recruited more or less casually for a specific commission and paid off when it was over, sailors had become permanent members of a military fighting service. When sail gave way to steam, life on board ship became easier, but all seamen dreaded one particular chore demanded by steam power – coaling. Every man on board got covered and choked by coal dust loading coal into the ship's bunkers. Stokers and engine-room ratings made up roughly a third of a typical warship's crew. Another third – seamen and signal ratings – made up what was termed the executive branch, providing the manpower to work the ship and load and fire its guns.

IN CASE OF EMERGENCY
Royal Navy sailors practise their lifeboat drill (left). The Navy was immensely conservative, even when it came to saving life. The sailors here are lowering the lifeboat the old-fashioned way, manually with ropes, rather than using the mechanical device. Just two years after this peace-time picture was taken, the Royal Navy was called upon to transport troops to South Africa to fight in the Second Boer War. These cheering marines (right) are heading off to war on board the HMS *Niobe*, a Diadem-class cruiser recently completed at the Vickers works in Barrow.

'The navy is pretty good, but it's still full of spit and polish and fuss and muckings.'

Rudyard Kipling, letter to H W Gwynne, editor of the *Morning Post*, 1901

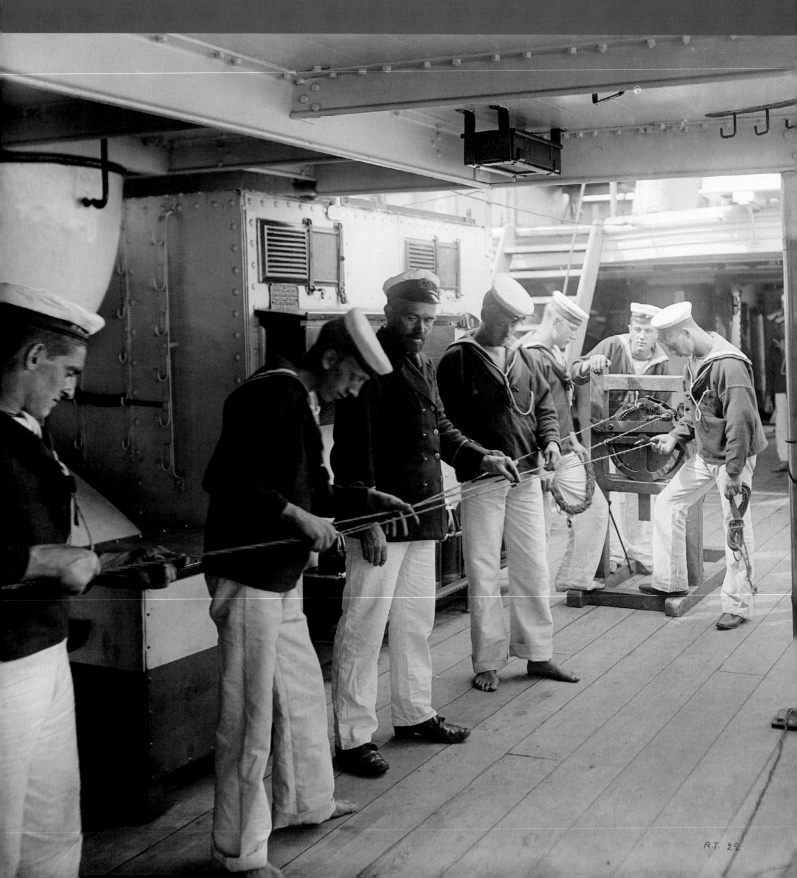

ON-BOARD HOUSEKEEPING
Barefoot sailors splice ropes on board ship, under the watchful eye of a warrant officer (left), while a sailmaker and his mate assiduously repair a damaged sail and some coir matting. Sail had given way to steam almost totally by the 1890s, a point acknowledged by Gilbert and Sullivan when they resurrected the gallant Captain Corcoran of *HMS Pinafore* as Captain Sir Edward Corcoran KCB in their 1893 comic opera *Utopia, Limited*. Sir Edward advises his listeners to 'unbend your sails, lower your yards and unstep your masts', but he concludes: 'Though we're no longer hearts of oak, Yet we can steer and we can stoke, And thanks to coal and thanks to coke, We never run a ship ashore!'

Technological progress might have transformed the navy, but, at heart, it was still rooted in deeply conservative traditions. More likely than not, this was because British supremacy at sea had been unchallenged from the conclusion of the Napoleonic Wars right up until the end of the 19th century. The only real action most sailors saw during this period came when the navy's battleships, cruisers, frigates and gun-boats were called on to carry out shore bombardments. There was no question of a head-to-head clash with an enemy fleet. Perhaps this was just as well, for many of the Royal Navy's hidebound admirals were stifled by tradition. Most of them certainly lacked the 'Nelson touch'. Throughout the service, showing imagination or taking any form of initiative was actively discouraged; what was expected was instant and unquestioning obedience to orders.

The Grand Old Man resigns

Both sides dug in their heels. Gladstone went on holiday, taking a villa in Biarritz. He was visited there by Sir Algernon West who found him as stubborn as ever, telling his visitor: 'You might as well try to blow up the Rock of Gibraltar'. Lord Acton, a personal friend, found him 'wild, violent, inaccurate … and governed by resentment'. When Gladstone again suggested calling an immediate general election, his ministers telegraphed back succinctly: 'Your suggestion is impossible.'

Things did not improve when Gladstone returned to London. Eventually, on 27 February, he wrote to the Queen, conveying 'the preliminary intimation' of his intention to resign. A few days later, he confided in the Cabinet and that same afternoon made what turned out to be his last speech in the House of Commons. He devoted it to an attack on the House of Lords. The next day, Gladstone formally tendered his resignation, giving as his reasons for retiring his failing eyesight and a general deterioration in his state of health.

A new political landscape

An era had ended. Out of all the great Victorian party political giants, only Salisbury was now active. The Queen immediately called on Rosebery to form a new government: 'She is fully aware of all the difficulties, but he is the only one of the Liberal Government in whom she has any real confidence and she earnestly presses him to undertake this task for a time, at least for her sake and for the good of the country.' Sir James Reid, the Queen's personal physician, urged Rosebery to accept the call for the sake of the Queen's health. 'She tells me that you are the only man of your party she likes and trusts', he confided, 'and that if you do not help in the present crisis, she does not know what she can do, as it would worry her beyond measure to have to fall back on anyone else.'

That was exactly what the Queen was determined to avoid. Gladstone was somewhat surprised not to be consulted about who should succeed him – had he been asked, he would have recommended Lord Spencer – but there was no constitutional necessity for the Queen to ask a retiring Prime Minister for advice. She was not prepared to consider Sir William Harcourt for the position. His bullying ways had upset her, as well as most of the Cabinet. 'He is a person I particularly dislike and cannot respect', she wrote to her eldest daughter, Victoria. Rosebery thought Harcourt 'a man of many qualities … all marred by a violent, uncontrollable temper'. Sir William agreed to soldier on as Chancellor and also to take on the Liberal leadership in the House of Commons, but before long the two men were barely on speaking terms, and Rosebery was as isolated as his predecessor had ended up being.

AGRICULTURAL DOLDRUMS

Away from the political mayhem of Westminster, the rhythms of the countryside continued as they had for centuries. This tranquil hay-making scene in the Lake District was photographed by Henry Mayson of Keswick. But the picture gives little hint of the hardships that farmers and farm labourers were suffering during the 1890s. In 1894, wheat prices fell to just 22s 10d a quarter – less than half the level they had been 20 years earlier. The results were tragic; thousands were forced off the land, joining the drift to the cities or the growing ranks of emigrants. Even big landlords felt the pinch. The novelist Rider Haggard was told by an acquaintance in Suffolk that some local landowners 'would be better off if they abandoned all attempts at agriculture … gave notice to their tenants and contented themselves with letting their shooting to South African millionaires'.

BUILDING FOR BUSINESS

Politics were not uppermost on everyone's minds as 1894 dawned. The Manchester Ship Canal – one of the last great feats of Victorian engineering – had finally been completed, linking that otherwise landlocked city directly with the Mersey estuary and the open sea beyond.

AROUND BRITAIN'S COASTS
The Clyde Shipping Company, the oldest concern of its kind in the world, ran steamship services from Glasgow to Ireland, London and the Channel ports. It was one of many similar companies that flourished in late Victorian Britain. But as Jerome K Jerome, author of *Three Men in a Boat*, warned, a short sea trip could be perilous: 'I remember my brother-in-law going for a short sea trip once for the benefit of his health. He took a return berth from London to Liverpool; and when he got to Liverpool, the only thing he was anxious about was to sell that return ticket. It was offered round the town at a tremendous reduction, so I am told; and was eventually sold to a bilious-looking youth who had just been advised by his medical men to go to the seaside, and take exercise.'

UNDER CONSTRUCTION
Workers at Walton Locks, near Warrington, pose for the camera during the building of the Manchester Ship Canal. The photograph was taken in about 1890, and the canal was completed in 1894. Walton Lock linked the canal to the upper reaches of the tidal River Mersey.

The Manchester Ship Canal

The canal opened to traffic on 1 January, 1894, a few months before its official opening and with work still continuing. It was nonetheless a memorable occasion. Sir Bosdin Leech, a former Lord Mayor of Manchester, described the procession of vessels setting out along the Canal for the first time: 'A mighty sound of cheering was given, but this was quickly drowned out by the combined efforts of scores of steam whistles and sirens. It was perfect pandemonium.'

It was the culmination of a long-cherished dream. For many years, it had been the ambition of Manchester businessmen to find a way of circumventing the stranglehold that Liverpool, in particular, held over the movement of goods to and from their city. Manchester was rightly nicknamed 'Cottonopolis'. Its flourishing

mills and those of the surrounding towns produced the finest cotton goods in the world. Yet its continued prosperity, some thought, was being endangered by factors outside the city's direct control. Some mill-owners complained that it was cheaper to send goods overland to Hull, on the other side of the country, than to transport them the 36 miles to Liverpool for shipping. The high costs began with the region's railways. A comparison with rates charged by rail networks around the country revealed that Manchester's industries were paying higher rail transportation costs than anywhere else. Then, when the goods reached Liverpool, the port authorities demanded their share in substantial harbour dues and levies. Manchester's businessmen were determined to break free from what they saw as economic servitude.

The answer seemed clear: build a canal to connect the city directly with the tidal waters of the Mersey estuary. The new sealink had to be big enough to be

'There is no doubt that Manchester is amply justified in her contention that the canal will give her a new lease of prosperity.'

Chambers Journal, 1889

WATER POWER
A camera captured the moment (left), reproduced in an albumen print, when water was let in at Ellesmere Port during construction. The ship canal was a massive undertaking, demanding the excavation and removal of millions of tons of soil and rock. The original engineers estimated that it would take four-and-a-half years to build and cost a little under £5 million. In the event, this overran to six years construction, while the cost more than tripled to more than £15 million. At the peak of building activity, some 16,000 men were employed, supported by more than 100 steam excavators, seven earth dredgers, 6,300 railway wagons, 173 locomotives and 124 steam cranes. When complete, the canal brought the benefits of extensive modern docks for ocean-going ships right into the heart of Manchester (below)

navigable by the largest sea-going vessels, so making Manchester not only a bustling industrial city but also a thriving port. But the scheme's promoters faced huge difficulties. First of all, parliamentary consent was needed to build the canal, and Parliament threw out the enabling legislation not once but three times before it was eventually passed. Then the promoters had to raise £5 million before construction could start. In addition, they had to buy out the Bridgewater Navigation Company, which controlled the existing waterways in the area. This cost them a further £1.71 million.

Eventually, in July 1887, some five years after the notion of a canal had first been seriously mooted, the necessary funds were in place. Four months later, on 11 November, Lord Egerton of Tatton, Chairman of the Manchester Ship Canal Company, ceremonially cut the first sod. Construction was underway.

The official opening of the Canal took place on 21 May, 1894. Queen Victoria journeyed north to perform the ceremony. Manchester City Council spent £10,000 decorating the streets and thousands turned out to join in celebrating the great day. A 21-gun artillery salute, fired from Manchester Racecourse, signalled the moment of opening. Festivities continued well into the night, culminating in a lavish state banquet and magnificent firework display.

HORSE POWER TO ELECTRIC POWER

A Hansom cab – the 'Gondola of London', according to Disraeli – at work in the City in the 1890s. Horses, whether pulling buses and trams, cabs for hire or private carriages, were still the mainstay of transport. But times were changing. The answer to the capital's transport problems, many thought, was to expand the underground railway.

The City & South London Railway opened in 1890, running from King William Street in the City to Stockwell, south of the Thames, with stations in between at Kennington, The Oval, Elephant & Castle and Borough. Plans were already afoot to extend the line both north and south. The C&SLR was the first deep underground railway in the world, and the first to run on electricity, using a third rail beneath the trains. The claustrophobic carriages were soon nicknamed 'padded cells', but it was popular nonetheless, carrying more than 5 million passengers in 1891. *Punch* christened it the 'sardine box railway'. The Waterloo & City Railway followed in 1898 and the Central London Railway two years later. The nucleus of the London Underground had been formed.

BLACKPOOL TOWER

In common with many other seaside resorts around Britain, Blackpool already had a pier. In fact, as the decade began it had two piers and was about to get a third, opened in 1893, at the southern end of its impressive sandy beach. Now, the Lancashire resort got something to make it stand out from the crowd – its very own version of the Eiffel Tower. The photographs here show the tower under construction in about 1893 (right), and shortly after completion (below) in an off-season view looking north from Blackpool's south beach.

Blackpool Tower was the brainchild of the town's mayor, John Bickerstaffe, and was designed by two local Lancashire architects, James Maxwell and Charles Tuke. Unlike the Parisian tower that inspired it, Blackpool Tower is not a freestanding structure; instead, its base is buried in buildings that contain facilities essential for a popular and ambitious seaside resort, including a ballroom and circus arena. The tower, which stands just over 518ft (158m) tall, took a little over two years to build and consumed more than 2,500 tons of iron and steel. It opened for business on 14 May, 1894, charging 6d for entry, plus another 6d to ride the lifts to the top, where on a fine day visitors could enjoy views stretching for more than 30 miles.

The tower soon became a central part of Blackpool's annual illuminations display, which had first bathed the promenade in 'artificial sunshine' as early as 1879. The sands, the tower and the many other attractions of the town pulled in thousands of visitors each year. The busiest time was Wakes Week, the traditional northern holiday when factories and mills closed down to give their workers a much-needed, albeit unpaid, week's break.

BLACKPOOL, SOUTH BEACH 1794

BUILDING TOWER BRIDGE

It took eight years to build Tower Bridge, but it had taken even longer to find a suitable design. The City of London Corporation had set up a special committee to decide what was to be done as far back as 1876. The big problem was how to build a bridge downstream from London Bridge without disrupting river traffic. More than 50 proposals were submitted and rejected. It was not until 1884 that Horace Jones, the

Corporation architect, and civil engineer John Wolfe Barry came up with a solution. Construction started two years later; this group shot (bottom left) shows some of the 432 construction workers involved.

What Jones and Barry had planned was a bascule bridge – the word comes from the French for see-saw. Two massive piers were sunk deep into the riverbed to support the construction, then more than 11,000 tons of steel were used to build the framework for the towers and walkways, all the time leaving a central gap to allow shipping to pass (top left). The piers and towers were clad in Cornish granite and Portland stone to protect the framework and to give the bridge a more pleasing appearance. The power from six massive pumping engines – stored until required in six giant accumulators – raised and lowered the bascules, which took around a minute to reach their maximum height. They were raised for the first time on 30 June, 1894, when the Prince and Princess of Wales performed the official opening ceremony amid a host of small boats (above). Not everyone was impressed with the design; an article in *The Builder* described it as the 'most monstrous and preposterous architectural sham we have ever known'.

WHEN COAL WAS KING

Coal kept the British economy turning in the 1890s. It was a major export and the Barry Railway and Docks in South Wales (right) were built specially for the shipping of Welsh coal. The industry depended on men like these, just returning to the surface after a shift at Frog Lane Pit near Bristol. When times became hard, however, the miners were among the first to suffer as colliery owners cut wages. In 1893, after a bitter strike of 11 weeks involving 250,000 miners, violence flared in the Yorkshire coalfields.

Police reinforcements and then troop detachments were sent in to restore order, with almost inevitable consequences. On 7 September, 1893, faced with an angry crowd outside the Ackton Hall Colliery, local magistrates read out the Riot Act. When the men did not disperse, magistrates ordered the troops to fire. Two men were killed and six wounded. A commission set up by Henry Asquith, the Home Secretary, to look into the incident concluded, predictably, that magistrates and troops were blameless.

BARRY DOCK & ISLAN

Wilde himself was 38. The pair quickly became inseparable and all sorts of rumours circulated about the exact nature of their relationship. Queensberry decided to do whatever it took to bring to an end what he saw as a totally unsuitable friendship. He forbade Lord Alfred ever to see Wilde again. Lord Alfred defied his father. When the furious Marquess called on the playwright to remonstrate with him, Wilde had him thrown out of his house.

Queensberry was not to be deterred. Calling at Wilde's club – Wilde and Douglas were on holiday together in Monte Carlo at the time – he left the playwright his visiting card, on which he had written, 'To Oscar Wilde posing as a Somdomite' [sic]. Wilde got the card, and the insult, on his return. Urged on by Lord Alfred, he decided to sue Queensberry for criminal libel.

The public was agog. The most popular dramatist of the day was suing one of its most colourful noblemen. Crowds flocked to hear the case. But things did not go as Wilde and Douglas had expected. Queensberry had spent a small fortune on private detectives to track down male prostitutes visited by Wilde and had them ready to give evidence. Moreover, he had hired Edward Carson, a celebrated abrasive barrister, to conduct his defence. Carson was acquainted with Wilde – they had been undergraduates together at Trinity College, Dublin – but any claim to friendship was left outside the court. Carson's ruthless cross-examination of Wilde destroyed all hope of his case succeeding. Sir Edward Clarke, Wilde's barrister, sought the judge's permission to withdraw the charge. Without even leaving the jury box, the jurors found Queensberry innocent.

The vengeful Marquess was not content with public vindication. He ordered his solicitors to pass all his evidence to the Director of Public Prosecutions. Wilde's arrest was duly ordered, though the magistrate issuing the warrant took care to give him time to catch the last Boat Train for the Continent. Despite the advice of many of his friends, Wilde chose to remain to stand trial. It ended with the jury failing to agree on a verdict, but in a second trial Wilde was found guilty and sentenced to two years' imprisonment with hard labour. His brilliant career was at an end. On his release, in 1897, Wilde took refuge in France under the pseudonym Sebastian Melmoth. He continued to write – *The Ballad of Reading Jail* appeared in 1898 – but he never recovered from his ordeal. He died in Paris in 1900.

FATAL ATTRACTION
Oscar Wilde with Lord Alfred 'Bosie' Douglas, his constant companion at the time of his greatest success (right). By the 1890s, Wilde had truly hit his stride as a writer. His novel *The Picture of Dorian Gray* appeared in 1890. *Lady Windermere's Fan* was first performed in 1892; this photograph (left) shows Marion Terry, sister of Ellen, in the title role. *A Woman of No Importance* followed in 1893, then *An Ideal Husband.* His masterpiece, *The Importance of Being Earnest*, opened at the St James's Theatre (top) on 14 February, 1895, to critical and public acclaim. It seemed Wilde could do no wrong, but events in his personal life were about to ruin him. Bosie's father, the eccentric Marquess of Queensberry, was determined to break up the friendship between Wilde and his son – and destroy Wilde into the bargain. He publicly accused the playwright of being a sodomite; Wilde responded with a law suit.

The case caused a sensation. Wilde started proceedings confidently enough, but it soon became clear that Queensberry had gathered a mass of incriminating evidence against him. Wilde found himself in the dock, charged with gross indecency. The public mood turned against him. In fear of the reaction, the St James's Theatre management closed *The Importance of Being Earnest* even before the guilty verdict was announced. One woman in the crowd outside the court shouted 'he'll have to have his hair cut proper now!'

SPLENDID
ISOLATION

Lord Salisbury's Conservatives won a landslide victory over the outgoing Liberals in the 1895 general election, but the massive majority did not mean that everything ran smoothly for the new Prime Minister. On the contrary, he faced major difficulties abroad. In Europe, his inability to pressurise the Turks to stop massacring Armenians brought home to him the limits of Britain's power. In South America, territorial claims by Venezuela on British Guiana won the backing of the USA. And in South Africa, Britain was heading for open war with the Boers. Canada's finance minister George Foster might eulogise about 'the great Mother Empire' standing 'splendidly isolated in Europe', but others argued that Britain needed to start finding some allies.

ALL THE WAY FROM OZ An Australian soldier, with his regimental mascot, in London for the Diamond Jubilee. Australians knew all about isolation, but being on the other side of the world allowed them a high degree of autonomy within the Empire.

A SHAKY START

Privately, Salisbury was mortified by his inability to put sufficient pressure on the Turks to stop the killing of Armenians, but his admirals had told him it was too risky to send the fleet through the Dardanelles. Publicly, there were plenty of critics to turn the screw. In September 1896 Gladstone came out of retirement to make a last stirring speech condemning the massacres, while David Lloyd George, a rising Liberal star, sneered that the Sultan was using British protests for cigarette papers. But it was the Liberal leader Lord Rosebery, not the Prime Minister, who became the biggest political casualty over the issue.

Rosebery had come to detest the premiership, but now he found the task of leading his party in opposition equally irksome. Even during the election campaign, he had failed to get the Liberal leaders to speak with one voice. Sir William Harcourt campaigned for temperance reform, John Morley spoke solely on Home Rule, both men totally ignoring Rosebery's attempt to make the House of Lords the central issue. Gladstone's passionate outburst over the Armenians was the final straw. Complaining that Gladstone's denunciation of the Turks enabled 'discontented Liberals to pelt me with your authority', Rosebery resigned as leader. Cynics said he had been looking for an excuse to do so for months.

Many regretted Rosebery's departure, but Sir William Harcourt was not one of them. In a letter to John Morley he wrote: 'I believe that he funked the future which he saw before him – that he felt called upon to say something on politics in general and give a lead and that he did not know what to say and so he took up his hat and departed.' Arthur Balfour, now Leader of the House of Commons, was more succinct. On hearing the news, he told Margot Asquith, wife of the former Liberal Home Secretary, that Rosebery was 'a bloody fool'.

DIAMONDS AND GOLD
The Bultfontein Diamond Mine, just outside Kimberley, in 1888. The South African diamond and gold fields drew men in their thousands seeking their fortune, and turned South Africa into one of the richest territories in the British Empire. The problem, as Lord Salisbury, the British Prime Minister (left), was to discover, was the fact that the Boers, not the British, were in charge in the Transvaal where the gold was located. The Boers had won their autonomy in the settlement that ended the First Boer War, back in the 1880s. Now, they jealously guarded that independence. They called the miners – many of them British citizens – *uitlanders* (outsiders), and while refusing them any political rights, they taxed them to the hilt. The *uitlanders* protested about unfair treatment, but when Dr Jameson, Cecil Rhodes's chief lieutenant, led an armed incursion to help them, they proved unwilling and unable to fight.

CECIL RHODES – COLONIAL DREAMS

The empire-builder Cecil Rhodes – seen above in a photograph taken at his South African home in 1890 and (above right) earlier in his career with officers of a Scottish regiment – made his fortune from diamond and gold-mining in South Africa. Born in Bishop's Stortford, Hertfordshire, in 1853, he was a sickly, asthmatic child. His parents sent him to join his brother in the Cape in 1870, in the hope that the climate would be good for his health. He soon began to make his mark. In the 1880s he founded the De Beers mining company and entered South African politics. In 1890 he became Prime Minister of the Cape Colony.

One of Rhodes's ambitions was to create a British route from the Cape to Cairo. 'Africa', he told Parliament, 'is ... lying ready for us. It is our duty to take it.' The cartoon of him bestriding the continent appeared in *Punch* after he announced plans for a Cape-to-Cairo telegraph. In pursuit of his dream to paint the African map British pink, his British South Africa Company won control of

Matabeleland and Mashonaland; the new country was eventually named after him – Rhodesia. It was the Boers who proved his undoing. Deeply implicated in the disastrous Jameson Raid into the Transvaal in 1895, he was forced to resign the Cape premiership.

Rhodes died of heart failure in 1902, aged just 49. His reported last words were 'so little done, so much to do'. He was buried in the Matopa Hills, Rhodesia, in a traditional burial site of African chiefs. He is seen here (far right) on a visit there in 1897. Dr W T Gaul, the Bishop of Mashonaland, conducted his funeral, reading a poem by Rudyard Kipling written specially for the occasion. Three chieftains and 2,000 tribesmen were among the many mourners. After the ceremony, the *New York Times* reported, they 'supplemented the Christian interment rites in their own fashion by the sacrifice of fifteen oxen to the shade of the great dead chief'. Dr Leander Starr Jameson was buried alongside his old friend and colleague after the First World War.

THE RHODES COLOSSUS

'Having done by their blundering folly as great a disservice as it was possible to render, not only to the *Uitlanders* but to the best interests of the Empire … [the Jameson raiders] were, on their arrival in England, acclaimed and feted … as the worthy successors of Drake and Raleigh.'

Henry Asquith, Liberal Home Secretary, criticising the Jameson Raid

CHANGING TIMES

For the leader of a political party that openly espoused the imperialist cause, Salisbury was no jingo. Indeed, he despised jingoism as the 'bastard brother' of true patriotism. He had a particular dislike of the new popular press, arguing that their super-patriotism was doing infinite damage to Britain's relationships with foreign powers. Salisbury had Alfred Harmsworth's *Daily Mail* in his sights as the prime example of what he had in mind.

Founded in 1896, the *Daily Mail* revolutionised British popular journalism. Harmsworth's career as a press magnate had begun in 1888, when, with his brother Harold, he launched a new magazine titled *Answers to Correspondents*. Within four years, it was selling more than a million copies a week. He went on to establish *Forget-Me-Knots*, a woman's magazine, and *Comic Cuts*, a children's paper aimed mainly at boys. Both ventures were just as successful.

The next step was to get involved in newspapers proper. In 1894, Harmsworth purchased the virtually moribund *Evening News*, which despite its proud claim to have 'the largest circulation of any evening paper in London' was fast approaching bankruptcy. Harmsworth dramatically changed the look of the paper and the way it presented news – and transformed its fortunes. By 1896, it had a daily circulation approaching 800,000 and was making a profit of £50,000 a year.

The stage was set for Harmsworth's boldest venture. On 4 May, 1896, the first issue of the *Daily Mail* hit the streets. It cost just a halfpenny, at a time when most

MEDIA MOGUL WITH A MIDAS TOUCH
Together with his brother Harold, the publishing magnate Alfred Harmsworth (right) created a hugely successful newspaper empire. At its peak, it included the *Daily Mail, Evening News, Daily Mirror, Sunday Dispatch, The Observer, The Times* and the *Sunday Times*. Their first paper was the *Evening News*, which boasted in its slogan that it was always 'first with the news'. The *Daily Mail*, launched in 1896, was an instant hit. The 30-year-old Harmsworth claimed that it was the ideal 'Busy man's journal'. It was also sold as great value for money – another Harmsworth slogan claimed that readers were getting 'a penny newspaper for a halfpenny'. By the start of the Boer War, the *Mail* had a circulation of more than a million, by far the highest of any newspaper in the world.

Among Salisbury's fellow bicycling enthusiasts were George Bernard Shaw and Sidney and Beatrice Webb – it must have been one of the few things that the Tory Prime Minister had in common with the left-wing leaders of the Fabian Society. But Salisbury had a pragmatic reason for taking up his new hobby. He had to do something about his weight. Urged on by his doctors, who were concerned by his increasingly corpulent state, he purchased a stately Humber tricycle and henceforth, wearing a purple poncho, could be seen out cycling along Pall Mall and Birdcage Walk of a morning. The imposing machine, supplied and serviced by the British Pattison Hygienic Saddle Company of New Bond Street, had a step at its back for a footman to stand on when it went downhill.

Salisbury liked the activity, but with one reservation. 'He thoroughly enjoys his exercise', Lord Balcarres, a guest at Hatfield House, the premier's imposing country home, noted, 'but is always in terror lest he be ambushed by some of the numerous grandchildren who all think him fair game.' He had zigzag paths laid through the undulating parkland around the house to create more tolerable cycling conditions. It took some effort to complete the task; one particularly deep cutting required the removal of nearly 500 tons of gravel to enable the Prime Minister to continue peddling gravely along.

TWO WHEELERS
Leisure cyclists parade in a London park, watched by a crowd of onlookers. In March 1896 it was reported that, on pleasant mornings, up to 3,000 cyclists could be seen enjoying a brisk pedal beside the Serpentine in Hyde Park. Cycling really took off as a recreational activity during the 1890s, with membership of the Cycling Touring Club passing 60,000. It was a hobby that people of all classes and ages could enjoy. A host of specialist magazines sprang up to cater for this new audience, including *Cycling Magazine* which in 1896 claimed to be selling more than 41,000 copies. Before long, dressmakers were offering women outfits specially designed for cycling (right). Whether or not she knew it, the lady in this small family party (far right) was following the fashion advice of *Women's World*, which recommended 'a plain sailor straw or a felt hat'.

QUICKER BY TRAIN
Liverpool Street Station bustles with activity as Victorian commuters pour off the suburban platforms. The railways were fast, cheap and reliable and practically everyone in late Victorian times travelled by train at some point – for cyclists it was a popular way of getting out into the country for a day's riding. Then, as the final full decade of Victoria's reign neared its end, a fledgling rival emerged. It would be years before the car challenged the supremacy of the train, but its presence would soon be felt.

STRANGE DESIGN
Victor Ashby is pictured below at the tiller of a Coventry Motette, a strange-looking three-wheeler that was manufactured by the Great Horseless Carriage Company in Coventry between 1896 and 1899. Originally a French design, the vehicle looks like a cross between a car and a motorcycle. Ashby soon started making his own cars. The first one, called the 'Jigger', was intended for family use and was powered by a twin-cylinder engine that Ashby designed and built himself.

THE ARRIVAL OF MOTOR CARS

Cycling was something everyone could enjoy. The better-off working class could easily afford machines, especially as hire purchase terms were readily available. Motoring, by contrast, was a pastime only the rich could afford. Motor cars were put on public display for the first time in Britain at a Crystal Palace exhibition in 1896. People flocked, spellbound, to see the new machines.

TO THE NOBILITY & GENTRY
MAY 1896

THE GREAT HORSELESS CARRIAGE

HAS THE HONOUR TO PRESENT

This NOVEL vehicle is propelled by an
INTERNAL COMBUSTION ENGINE
OF 2 CYLINDERS AND 6 HORSE POWER,
relying on petroleum for its motive force

THE MECHANICAL carriage
will attain the comfortable speed of
TWELVE MILES PER HOUR
on the level, while hills can be ascended
and descended in safety

The Daimler
is admirably suited

SPORT
AND LOVER OF TH
giving as it does
the enjoy
FRESH AIR
UNINTERRUPTED VI

THE TWIN-CYLINDER 6 H.P. WAGONETT

ROLLS WITHOUT ROYCE

The Hon Charles Rolls, who later founded
Rolls-Royce with engineer Henry Royce, is
seen cautiously driving his first car (top), a
3.75hp Peugeot he imported from France.
By 1898 Rolls was happily at the wheel of a
Panhard-Levassor racer (left). That same
year, another Panhard was photographed
on the road during the first Automobile
Club rally (right). In 1896, The Great
Horseless Carriage Company (above),
brainchild of entrepreneur Harry Lawson,
became the first British company to build a
motor car, albeit to a French design. The
next year, the first Daimler car appeared.

The Locomotives on the Highway Act, which Parliament passed that same year, helped to stimulate motoring enthusiasm. It did away with the need for motor vehicles to be preceded by a man on foot and was popularly christened the 'Red Flag Act'. In fact, the requirement for the pedestrian to carry a red warning flag had been done away with 18 years before. Nevertheless, the passing of the new act sparked a motoring revolution and enthusiasts celebrated by taking their cars on an 'emancipation run' from London to Brighton.

Then, as now, the motor car divided opinion. Queen Victoria was not an enthusiast. 'I'm told', she commented, 'that they smell exceedingly nasty and are very shaky and disagreeable.' Predictably, the Prince of Wales was of the opposite view. He took his first drive while a guest at Warwick Castle and was impressed. 'The motor car', he said, 'will become a necessity for every English gentleman.'

'A rush at full speed in a motor car over a lonely road, and through a deserted country, wide and open, is an experience to be ever after remembered.'

J J Hissey, travel writer

THE EMANCIPATION RUN

The Locomotives on Highways Act of 1896 raised the speed limit for what it quaintly termed 'light locomotives' from 4 to 14mph and did away with the requirement for a man to walk in front of a moving car. To celebrate, the newly founded Motor Car Club organised the first London to Brighton car rally on 14 November, 1896. The event was billed as 'the first legal run of the New Automotive Carriages in England', but it quickly became known as the Emancipation Run. The rally attracted 33 intrepid pioneers who set off from the Hotel Metropole in London to drive the 60 miles of rough road to Brighton. Only 14 made it to the Hotel Metropole on Brighton's sea front, where the rally ended.

ON THEIR WAY
Despite blustery weather, enthusiastic crowds turned out on the day (left). Before the cars set off Lord Winchilsea, a prominent patron of the Motor Car Club, ceremonially burned a red flag to symbolise the liberation of motoring. Then, according to one observer, things 'started in confusion and ended in chaos'. The cars made their way slowly south through the suburbs (above), and out onto the London to Brighton road. There were no actual accidents, but many breakdowns along the way. It was even rumoured that one of the finishing cars was secretly conveyed to Brighton by train, then hastily covered with mud before puffing its way across the finishing line.

THE FINISHING LINE

Most of the participants in the Emancipation Run were in French vehicles, the French having enthusiastically embraced the motor car years before the British. These two mud-spattered vehicles on the finishing line outside Brighton's Hotel Metropole are both Panhard-Levassors. Frenchmen Rene Panhard and Emile Levassor built their first car in 1890; by 1896, the cars they designed were widely recognised as market leaders. They were the first car manufacturer, for instance, to position the engine at the front. However, they were not the first vehicles to cross the finishing line in November 1896. That honour belonged to a tiny Bollee three-wheeler, and another one took second place. They were driven by the Bollee brothers, two more Frenchmen who designed and built their own machines.

For most people, buying and running a car was an impossible ambition. Not only were they prohibitively expensive, they required a chauffeur to drive them and many manufacturers recommended the employment of a travelling engineer to deal with the inevitable breakdowns. Nevertheless, motoring rapidly grew in popularity. Among those bitten by the bug was the poet and writer Rudyard Kipling. He had his first outing in a car in 1898, courtesy of Alfred Harmsworth who had travelled down to Rottingdean in Sussex, where Kipling was living at the time, 'in one of those motor-car things' specially for the purpose. After an excursion lasting just 20 minutes – from which the poet and his wife 'returned white with dust and dizzy with noise' – Kipling was converted. Within two months, he had hired a car of his own, complete with driver, from a Brighton motor-car agency, at a cost of three-and-a-half guineas a week.

THE DIAMOND JUBILEE

On 23 September, 1896, Queen Victoria wrote in her journal: 'Today is the day on which I have reigned longer, by a day, than any English sovereign.' The telegrams of congratulation started pouring into Balmoral Castle, her Scottish retreat, where she was entertaining the young Tsar Nicholas II of Russia and his new bride, Alexandra, but she cautioned well-wishers against premature celebration. 'People want to make all sorts of demonstrations', she noted, 'which I asked them not to do until I had completed the sixty years next June.'

In fact, planning for the Diamond Jubilee had already begun. Two decisions set the occasion apart from the Golden Jubilee celebrations a decade previously. Firstly, in view of Victoria's age, it was proposed that the programme of events should be less demanding than it had been ten years before. Secondly, no reigning monarchs were to be invited. Instead, on the suggestion of Joseph Chamberlain, pride of place would be given to the Prime Ministers of Britain's colonies; some would have places in the procession, while for others special seating would be provided outside St Paul's, where a grand service of thanksgiving was to be held. The Indian princes were also encouraged to attend – many did so and made a great impression in their bejewelled finery.

The Queen happily fell in with both suggestions, though she did insist on issuing a personal invitation to her cousin, the King of the Belgians, and his younger daughter. Nor did the lack of invitations to reigning monarchs deter sundry princes, grand dukes and other notable royals – from Russia, Naples, Prussia, Wurttemberg, Saxony, Luxembourg, Hesse, Bavaria and Austria – from flooding into the country, all determined to join in the fun.

The great day dawns

The proceedings started with a family service in St George's Chapel, Windsor, on Sunday, 20 June, 1897. It was timed to coincide with celebratory services held at other places of worship all over the country.

The music for the service had been chosen with great care. The choir was to sing a *Te Deum* composed many years before by Prince Albert, after which a special Jubilee hymn, set to music by Sir Arthur Sullivan, the Queen's favourite composer, was to be performed. The hymn had produced one of the Jubilee's few hiccups. When Alfred Austin, the new poet laureate, submitted his words for the hymn to Sullivan, the composer rejected them as unsuitable. Luckily, the Prince of Wales solved the problem by persuading Walsham Howe, the Bishop of Wakefield, to hastily write an alternative.

Later on in the day, the Queen left Windsor for Buckingham Palace. There, the following evening, she hosted a lavish state banquet attended by Lord Salisbury and members of the Cabinet, as well as scores of other notables. In honour of the happy occasion, the Queen did not wear black for the first time in all her long years of widowhood. She retired relatively early to get a good night's rest and prepare herself for the actual Jubilee day.

SIXTY GLORIOUS YEARS
Queen Victoria poses for her official Diamond Jubilee photograph (left). *Graphic Magazine* chose to feature a portrait of the young Victoria on the cover of its special anniversary edition (above). The Queen had been looking forward to her special day for months and enjoyed the celebrations immensely. They were marred only by her chronic lumbago, which made it impossible for her to get out of her carriage and climb the steps into St Paul's, where a great commemoration service was held. Instead, she had to be content to listen to the proceedings from outside the cathedral. 'I was unfortunate,' she later told the Bishop of Winchester, 'I had a very bad place and saw nothing.'

GREAT REJOICING

On Jubilee Day, hundreds of thousands of cheering citizens lined the streets to watch the royal cavalcade on its way from Buckingham Palace to St Paul's, and on its return route which went south of the river. Countless loyal citizens spent precious savings on a souvenir of the occasion – a mug, a plate, or perhaps playing cards with the Queen's picture (above).

Victoria rode in an open carriage (right), with the Prince of Wales and her grandson Kaiser Wilhelm II on horseback immediately behind her. Some 50,000 troops took part in the display. Alfred Austin, the poet laureate, composed a poem for the occasion. The Queen was practically the only person who liked it. It was called simply 'Victoria' and ran to 30 stanzas, ending with the lines:

> And ever, when mid-June musk roses
>   blow,
> Our race will celebrate Victoria's name,
> And ever England's greatness gain a
>   glow,
> From our pure fame.

The artist Edward Burne-Jones recorded his rather mixed impressions of the day. 'It was all surprisingly successful, but all the boasting of the papers is so dreadful; it makes one wonder that a thunderbolt doesn't fall upon London … the gods do not love the pride of cockiness. And all this enthusiasm spent over one little unimportant old lady in the one effort of imagination of the English race. It's curious, but rather pretty.'

Celebrating Jubilee Day

At first, the skies were overcast, but the sun soon broke through the clouds. It was 'Queen's weather', many said as they flocked to line the six-mile route that the royal procession was to take from Buckingham Palace to St Paul's and back. On the return, after the service, the parade crossed London Bridge and travelled south of the Thames, returning to the palace via Westminster Bridge, Parliament Square, Horse Guards Parade and The Mall. An estimated million people turned out to salute the Queen as she passed. All seemed, she said, 'delighted to see their little old Queen'. Waving flags were everywhere, while even the buildings were emblazoned with loyal slogans: 'One Race, One Queen' and 'God Bless Our Sovereign'. Lilywhites, the Piccadilly sporting goods store, went with a cricketing theme: 'Her Gracious Majesty's Grand and Glorious Innings, 60 Not Out!'

Promptly at 11.15am, cannons boomed out in Hyde Park to signal the Queen's departure from the palace. Before she left, she pressed a special button to despatch a telegraph message to the myriad peoples of the empire. It read simply: 'From my heart, I thank my beloved people. May God bless them.'

The procession slowly wound its way through Westminster and on into the City of London. The Queen drove in an open landau, accompanied by the Princess of Wales and Princess Helena, her third daughter. According to the inveterate diarist Lady Monkswell, 'she was sitting quite upright and brisk in the carriage, not looking flushed or overcome, but smiling and bowing. She was dressed in grey and black, and held in her hand the very long-handled black lace parasol lined with white, given her by Mr Charles Villiers, the oldest MP. She held it high up so that we could see her face.'

The crowds cheered the Queen every step of the way – cries of 'Go it, old girl' were heard. Some 50,000 troops took part in the procession, led by Field Marshall Lord Roberts mounted on his favourite Arab pony. It was the largest military force ever assembled in the capital. Lady Monkswell left a vivid record of what she saw: 'First came the Naval Brigade with guns and then ten or twelve colonial premiers and their wives in carriages, each followed by the mounted troops of their colony, such strange, fine looking horsemen. The excellent premiers and their wives, who in their continent are quite small people, had never had such a good day in their lives, and were chiefly grinning from ear to ear with joy and pride. They were very well cheered.'

There was much more for Lady Monkswell to report: 'Secondly came Captain Ames, the tallest man in the British Army, 6 feet 8 inches, and his four troopers, seven or eight batteries of Horse Artillery, divided by what seemed to my aching sight endless squadrons of Dragoon Guards, Hussars, the Scots Greys, and the 17th Lancers. Thirdly, came the splendid troops of native Indian Cavalry, the Indian princes in their magnificent native costumes and riding the most splendid horses. The last, riding alone, was Sir Pertan Singh, ADC to the Prince of Wales and the great polo player. He looked one mass of gold.'

The Queen was visibly affected. As the acclamations mounted, she was moved to tears. 'How kind they are', she repeated over and over again as the Princess of Wales leaned forward in the carriage to pat her hand in congratulation. Later, she wrote in her journal: 'No one ever, I believe, has met with such an ovation as was given to me passing through those six miles of streets. The crowds were quite indescribable and their enthusiasm really marvellous and deeply touching. The cheering was quite deafening, and every face seemed to be filled with real joy.'

AROUND THE COUNTRY
Jubilee celebrations took place the length and breadth of the country. Here, loyal citizens of Northampton gather at the town's racecourse to pay their tribute to the Queen. In the village of Amberley in Sussex, the villagers organised a gala sports day to honour the great occasion. It ended with the National Anthem 'to be sung by everyone', according to the official programme for the day.

St Paul's and after

The Prime Minister, Lord Salisbury, with his wife and the entire Cabinet stood waiting on the steps of St Paul's Cathedral for the Queen's arrival. They were not alone. Two military bands, members of the Diplomatic Corps, senior clergy, 500 choristers, a detachment of Yeomen of the Guard and the Gentlemen at Arms were also in close attendance. As the royal carriage drew up in the bright sunshine, the *Te Deum* and the Hundredth Psalm were sung. When Frederick Temple, the venerable Archbishop of Canterbury, called on the crowd to give the Queen three cheers, the response could be heard all the way to Trafalgar Square.

It was an unforgettable moment for all who witnessed it. Lady Monkswell summed up her own feelings: 'When she was passed and we felt we had done our Jubilee, I had an over-powering emotion of thankfulness and satisfaction that I, with husband and sons, had been present at this great, this tremendous occasion.' The Prime Minister was just as moved. That evening he wrote to the Queen: 'It [the Jubilee] will live in history as a unique and unexampled demonstration of the attachment which has grown more and more in intensity between the sovereign of a vast Empire and her subjects in every clime.' Characteristically, the Prince of Wales was more succinct: 'All', he said, 'had gone off splendidly.'

IMPERIAL VISITORS
Colonial troops in Britain for the Jubilee pose with some young admirers. The troops received a warm welcome. They were admitted free to all the theatres, and the great actor Sir Henry Irving gave a special afternoon performance in their honour. Queen Victoria hosted a luncheon for the officers in St George's Hall, Windsor Castle. 'It was a great sight', recalled one Canadian. 'We ate off silver plate and were waited on by footmen in scarlet coats ...' Afterwards, Victoria reviewed the troops in Windsor Great Park, when the same Canadian had the chance to observe her closely: 'I stood only a few feet from the royal carriage ... She appeared to be in good health, but naturally looked old. Her face was full and little wrinkled. Her complexion was rosy, but she was very short-sighted, wearing heavy concave glasses.'

The empire celebrates

Outside the capital, every city, town and village in the land hosted parties of one sort or another. Between Caithness and Land's End 2,500 beacons blazed to commemorate the occasion. Manchester City Council spent £10,000 on street decorations and also paid for a breakfast party for 100,000 children. In Inverness, crowds gathered outside the Town House to celebrate in song. The banners decorating the Town House above their heads were inscribed in Gaelic – the English translation read: 'As long as Clachnacuddin exists, Victoria's illustrious character will endure in our memory.'

The celebrations were empire-wide. Across the Atlantic, in far away Winnipeg, newspapers claimed the occasion 'showed how patriotism can bind in joyous and fraternal bonds elements of every nation and creed'. In the Indian province of Hyderabad, every tenth prisoner was set free.

Perhaps strangest of all, Oscar Wilde gave a Jubilee party in Dieppe, his first place of exile to which he had fled following his release from prison. He later

FROM FAR AND WIDE
Soldiers from every part of the empire came to the mother country to take part in the Jubilee celebrations to honour the Queen. Some of the colonial infantry seemed half-crippled by their boots, which they were unaccustomed to wearing. One Maori rifleman weighed in at 28 stones, while a Dyak from Borneo, so it was reported, had taken 13 human heads before joining the colours. The author J E C Bradley later noted that it was only at the Diamond Jubilee that 'the imperial idea, which had long been growing in the nation, first touched the imagination of the populace, as it cheered the citizen-soldiery of young colonies guarding the venerable mother of all the Britains.'

'It is known to all the people of this country, it is known to all the peoples of the vast Empire over which she rules, that there is no-one throughout that Empire who could have inspired more universal respect … than the Queen who presides over us.'

Earl of Kimberley, House of Lords, 21 June, 1897

THE SPLENDOUR OF PRINCES
Members of the Indian contingent at Queen Victoria's Jubilee garden party at Buckingham Palace. The Indian princes and cavalry officers had made an immediate impression on the watching crowds on Jubilee day. The diarist Lady Monkswell recorded that they were in 'magnificent native costumes and riding the most splendid horses'. The only regret was that relatively few of them took part, but as Lord George Hamilton, Secretary of State for India, explained to the House of Commons, such a move would be 'attended by almost insuperable difficulties.'

wrote to Lord Alfred Douglas: 'My fete was a huge success: fifteen gamins were entertained on strawberries and cream, apricots, chocolates, cakes and sirop de grenadine. I had a huge iced cake with Jubile de la Reine Victoria in pink … and a great wreath of red roses round it all. Every child was asked beforehand to chose his present: they all chose instruments of music!!! They sang the Marseillaise and other songs, and danced a ronde, and also played God Save the Queen. They said it was God Save the Queen, and I did not like to differ from them. They also all had flags which I gave them. They were most gay and sweet.'

Nothing could have been a greater contrast than the great fancy dress ball given by the Duke and Duchess of Devonshire at Devonshire House in London at the start of July. Without question, it was the most elaborate entertainment of the entire Jubilee summer. The Duke himself sported the Collar and Badge of the Golden Fleece, which the Prince of Wales lent him for the occasion. The Duchess was dressed as Zenobia, Queen of Palmyra. Perhaps the most striking guest was Princess Henry of Hess, who came as the Queen of Sheba, her long train borne aloft by four negro pageboys.

The end of an epoch

The celebrations seemed endless. On 26 June, the Princess of Wales hosted a banquet for 400,000 of London's poorest inhabitants, at which a mammoth 700 tons of food was consumed. The same day, her husband reviewed the fleet at Spithead, sailing past 21 battleships, 53 cruisers, 30 destroyers and 24 torpedo boats, all drawn up at anchor in two lines 25 miles long. Britannia, it seemed clear, really did rule the waves. It was a show of strength no other nation in the world could come near matching. George Goschen, the First Lord of the Admiralty, was proud to point out that the great armada had been assembled without recourse to recalling any ships stationed in the Pacific, the Mediterranean or in the North Atlantic.

Of all the celebratory events attended by the Queen, she particularly enjoyed a march-past of some 4,000 boys, all handpicked representatives from the cream of the country's public schools. They cheered the Queen to the echo as they passed the reviewing stand; the Queen said that she thought the boys from Eton and Harrow looked rather smarter than the rest. Another was the garden party she hosted at Buckingham Palace towards the end of Jubilee month. The indefatigable Lady Monkswell once again recorded her impressions of the scene.

'Indian cavalry officers were there in great numbers, splendid men in handsome uniforms and long boots. The Queen got into a large Victoria drawn by two greys … She went all around the garden, everybody crowding round and curtseying in a way which must have satisfied her inmost heart. She then went and sat in a large tent banked up with flowers; it was wide open – all the front – and her faithful subjects could see her taking her tea and having her toast buttered by the Indian servant.'

Lord Robert Cecil, one of Lord Salisbury's sons, described the great Jubilee as 'the climax of the Victorian Age. England had never been so powerful'. Others were not so sure. The Radical writer J W Mackail wrote to Rudyard Kipling of his fear that the country was heading for a 'big smash'. Kipling replied: 'The big smash is coming one of these days sure enough, but I think we shall pull through not without credit.' He added presciently: 'It will be the common people – the third-class carriages – that'll save us.'

BACK TO
BUSINESS

After the excitement of the Jubilee, life returned briefly to normal. In London there was a special attraction to enjoy – Barnum and Bailey's Circus, 'the greatest show on Earth'. Nothing quite like it had been seen in Britain before. Meanwhile, in the Sudan, Lord Kitchener was advancing up the Nile to retake Khartoum. It was a great imperial triumph, but the following year, when war broke out in South Africa, the army stumbled into a series of disasters. Nevertheless, spirits remained high. The Queen spoke for her people when she told Arthur Balfour: 'Please understand that there is no one depressed in this house; we are not interested in the possibilities of defeat; they do not exist.'

WILLING VOLUNTEER When the Boer War broke out Sir Arthur Conan Doyle, the creator of Sherlock Holmes, tried to enlist as a soldier, but he was turned down as overage, overweight and unfit. Instead, he went out to South Africa to serve in the army as a doctor.

THE GREATEST SHOW ON EARTH

Britain had its own circuses, which had grown out of an older tradition of seasonal travelling fairs. But it had never seen anything on the scale of what Barnum and Bailey billed as 'the world's largest, grandest, best amusement institution'. The tour of Britain in 1898 was organised like a military operation. Four special trains, each pulled by three locomotives, were required to transport the 300 performers, 400 horses, 20 elephants, Johanna the Giant Gorilla and the show's many other 'curious creatures and creations'. In all, the circus employed some 800 people. Jumbo the Elephant, seen here with his trainer Matthew Scott at London Zoo, had been bought by Barnum for his circus some years before. Many were heartbroken to see him go; 100,000 schoolchildren signed a petition to the Queen, asking her to stop the sale. Sadly, Jumbo – described by Barnum as 'the towering monument of his mighty race' – was not part of the tour: he had been killed charging a train in North America.

'RECESSIONAL' THOUGHTS AND JINGOIST VOICES

Not everyone was as optimistic as the Queen. Even at the height of the Jubilee year, some had attempted to sound a note of caution. Chief among them was Rudyard Kipling, the Empire's most famous story-teller. To mark the occasion he wrote a poem that he titled 'Recessional', in which the celebratory tones were tinged with sombre foreboding.

Kipling's poem was published in *The Times* on 17 July, 1897, just before the Jubilee celebrations proper were due to start. Looking ahead to a time when 'The tumult and the shouting dies: The Captains and the Kings depart,' Kipling warned that what *The Times,* in its accompanying editorial, termed the 'most dangerous and demoralising temper … [of] boastful pride' might lead to national disaster:

> 'Far-called, our navies melt away;
> On dune and headland sinks the fire:
> Lo, all our pomp of yesterday
> Is one with Nineveh and Tyre!
> Judge of the Nations, spare us yet,
> Lest we forget – lest we forget!'

Coming from Kipling, a leading proponent of the imperial ideal and far from being a pacifist, such sentiments were a surprise. Kipling himself was in two minds about the poem. He began it on 22 June, then put it aside while he went to sea on board a Channel Fleet cruiser taking part in naval exercises. On his return he sent the draft to fellow-writer Rider Haggard, expressing his concern that 'it may be quoted as an excuse for lying down abjectly at all times and seasons and taking what any other country may think fit to give us'. He went so far as to throw the poem into his wastepaper basket, but two friends rescued it and persuaded him to revise it for publication. When it appeared in print, it caused a sensation.

Alone or with allies

Lord Salisbury had some sympathy with Kipling's dilemma. In February 1898, in the debate on the Queen's Speech following the State Opening of Parliament, he warned listening peers and MPs against the dangers of encouraging imperial overreach. 'However strong you may be, whether you are a man or a nation', he said, 'there is a point beyond which your strength will not go. It is madness. It ends in ruin if you allow yourself to pass beyond it.'

It was not an opinion shared by all in the House. Some of Salisbury's own Cabinet disagreed with him. At the time, the Chinese Empire seemed to be tottering inexorably towards disintegration, and most saw no reason why Britain should not be scrambling for a share of the spoils.

Pressure on the government to act in the Far East mounted. When the Russian fleet steamed into Port Arthur (today's Lüshun, in China's northeastern province of Liaoning) and Royal Navy warships in the area were obliged to withdraw, it was

BRITAIN'S BESTSELLER
Rudyard Kipling won instant fame as an author following the publication of his *Barrack-Room Ballads*. His captivating writings, such as *Plain Tales from the Hills* in which he depicted colourful aspects of life under the Raj in India, won him a ready audience, as did his enchanting tales for children, such as the *Just-So Stories* and *The Jungle Books*. He swiftly rose to literary prominence and became the most popular writer of both verse and prose throughout the English-speaking world. Edward Gosse, fellow-author and literary critic, wrote of Kipling's appeal: 'It is the strength of this new story-teller that he reawakens in us the primitive emotions of curiosity, mystery, and romance in action. He is the master of a new kind of terrible and enchanting peepshow, and we crowd around him begging for "just one more look".'

A POLITICAL ADMIRAL

For many years, Lord Charles Beresford successfully combined the roles of senior naval officer and Member of Parliament. He was a popular naval hero, having won lasting fame for his exploits during the Royal Navy's bombardment of Alexandria in 1892; he was promoted to vice-admiral in 1898. A mercurial Irishman, Beresford's quick temper made him a thorn in the side of Lord Salisbury's government. He pressed for an increase in naval expenditure far above anything that Salisbury was willing to consider. He was for years a close friend of the Prince of Wales, but they fell out over an incident involving Lady Daisy Brooke. At one time or other, Daisy – the real-life inspiration for the music hall song 'Daisy, Daisy' – was mistress to both men. She wrote a letter to Beresford, urging him to leave his wife for her, but Lady Beresford opened it in her husband's absence abroad. Lady Brooke appealed to the Prince to use his influence to have the letter returned. When Lady Beresford refused she was socially ostracised and her husband, furious at this treatment of his wife, the innocent party in the whole affair, threatened the Prince with public exposure. Though the scandal was hushed up, the Prince was affronted and upset by what he described as Beresford's 'base ingratitude after 20 years of friendship', and did not speak to him for many years.

seen as a national disgrace. Lord Charles Beresford, a senior naval officer turned politician, trumpeted loudly that the withdrawal was 'one of the most humiliating things that has happened in English history'. Robert Yerburgh, Conservative MP for Chester and a leader of the 'China Party' in the House of Commons, called on his fellow MPs to use their votes to 'avenge England's dishonour'.

It was bad enough that the MCC cricket team then touring Australia was being trounced – eventually it lost the series by four Test matches to one. Being shamed by the Russians on top of this was too much for people at home to bear. The clamour for action grew. In a speech at Cambridge, Sir William Harcourt, now the Liberal leader having succeeded Lord Rosebery, commented succinctly that 'the English people do not want to go to war, but they do not like being snubbed around the world'.

Lord Salisbury was determined not to be drawn into conflict. Instead, he came to terms with the Russians at China's expense. His government, having first taken up the offer of a lease on the port of Wei-hai-wei, now demanded the lease of more territory on the mainland adjacent to the island of Hong Kong. The Chinese had no alternative but to accede.

continued on page 123

ENVOY FROM THE EAST

Soldier turned diplomat Li Hung Chang was sent to Britain by the Dowager Empress of China to negotiate with Lord Salisbury and George Curzon, the Under-Secretary of State at the Foreign Office. As greedy and ambitious foreign powers sought to win concessions from the faltering Manchu regime in China, Li's objective was to establish what line the British government might take to help to resolve the China question. Li left Britain empty-handed, as Salisbury was not prepared to go to war against Russia to protect Chinese territorial integrity. Li also visited France, Russia and the USA on his diplomatic tour before returning home. In the USA, where he lodged a dignified protest against the continued ban on Chinese immigration, he impressed the Americans as a skilful negotiator: 'This heathen,' declared the *Boston Globe*, 'is giving our universal Yankee nation valuable points daily.'

THE BRITISH IN HONG KONG

A British lady, dressed in a loose gown suitable for the climate, takes the air out on deck in Hong Kong harbour in about 1895 (right). The panoramic view below, taken early in the morning, reveals Hong Kong's stuning natural harbour, which the British named Aberdeen Harbour after George Hamilton-Gordon, 4th Earl of Aberdeen. The port soon became a vital trading hub of the Empire, its streets – like Bonham Road (left) – bustling with business.

The island had been ceded to Britain in 1842, following China's defeat in the First Opium War. Kowloon, on the mainland, was added in 1860, then in 1899 the adjacent New Territories were granted on a 99-year lease from the Chinese government. Politicians were determined to maintain Britain's position in the Far East. George Curzon, Under-Secretary of State for Foreign Affairs, told the Commons: 'We were the first people to unlock the door of China to foreign trade; we were the first power to survey her coasts; we were the first to drive pirates from her seas. We were the first to stud the whole line of her coasts with ports open not only to ourselves, but to the commerce of the whole world.' This last boast was true and Hong Kong became the most prosperous port in the east under British rule.

'For myself, I am sure that, in the matter of science, Stoddart is unapproachable. It is wonderful to watch him when he pulls, to notice the effect this stroke, as he applies it, has upon the opposing bowlers, making them lose their line and their heads.'

Fred Spofforth, Australian fast bowler, 1896

PLAYING THE GAME

The end of the 19th century was a golden age for cricket: between 1891 and 1910, an average crowd of 14,000 spectators turned out to watch first-class county cricket. But this did not mean that the England side had all its own way in Test matches.

Andrew Stoddart (left) was the England captain and a favourite of the crowds. He was a splendid batsman, playing for Middlesex and England, and also played rugby for his country. Stoddart was chosen to lead the MCC side on their 1897-8 tour of Australia. It was his fourth cricketing trip there and his second as captain; the first had been in 1894 when the team – seen here on board ship on their outbound journey – returned successful. The 1897 team did not fare so well: England won the opening match, but Australia won the rest to take the series and the Ashes. In the second match, their fast bowler Ernie Jones had earned the dubious distinction of being the first player in Test history to be no-balled for throwing.

Stoddart did not take defeat well and he did not win any friends when he criticised the behaviour of the Australian crowds, complaining that his team had been put off by jeering from spectators. 'What I have said', he insisted, 'has been purely for the good of the game, for the sake of players in this country, and of English teams coming out here in the future.'

As far as Salisbury was concerned, honour was now satisfied, but Joseph Chamberlain, still the thrusting Colonial Secretary, was not content. When Kaiser Wilhelm II had telegrammed support to the Boers at the time of the Jameson Raid, Chamberlain had urged the premier to do something positive 'to soothe the wounded vanity of the nation'. Revealingly, he added: 'It does not matter which of our numerous foes we defy, but we ought to defy someone.'

Now, mindful of Salisbury's warning that Britain did not have enough guns to fight the Russians and the French together – Russia and France had concluded a military alliance in 1896 – Chamberlain believed he had the answer: an alliance with Germany. In spring 1898, without consulting the Prime Minister who was in the South of France recovering from influenza, Chamberlain met with Count Paul von Hatzfeldt, the German ambassador, and suggested that Britain and Germany should make an alliance.

When Salisbury heard of the discussions, he was dismissive. Britain, he told the Primrose League, was perfectly capable of standing on her own. 'We know that we shall maintain against all comers that which we possess,' he told his audience, 'and we know, in spite of the jargon about isolation, that we are amply competent to do so.' Chamberlain's great plan was stillborn.

The Colonial Secretary grumbled, but in the end gave way. And now, luckily for the government, a long-expected but nonetheless sad event happened which took people's minds off foreign affairs. Gladstone, the Grand Old Man of politics, died. 'The most distinguished political name in this century,' Salisbury announced to the House of Lords, 'has been withdrawn from the roll of the living.' He was, said the premier, the epitome 'of a great Christian statesman'.

THE DEATH OF GLADSTONE

Gladstone had been failing for some time, but the seriousness of his condition had not at first been recognised. He had cancer of a peculiarly malignant and painful type, which attacked first behind his cheekbone then slowly spread to other parts of his body. On 18 March, 1898, his doctors gave up hope and told him there was no possibility of recovery.

Gladstone spent the next two months in great pain, helped only by lavish doses of morphia and by listening to music. Towards the end, he became as quiet and gentle as a tired child, before passing into a state of semi-consciousness. He died without a struggle in the early hours of the morning on 19 May. Catherine, his wife of almost 60 years, and all his surviving children were at his bedside. The Reverend Stephen Gladstone, his second son, read the last prayers.

Immediately, the nation plunged into mourning. 'The deepest manifestations of grief are reported throughout the country', recorded the London correspondent of the *New York Times*. 'Flags are everywhere half-masted, the bells are tolling, shades are drawn down, and in the public galleries the pictures of Mr Gladstone have been draped with crepe.' Everyone seemed visibly moved.

LYING IN STATE
Members of the public file respectfully past Gladstone's coffin as it lies in state in Westminster Hall. Queues began to form as early as 2am; four hours later, the doors of the hall were opened and the procession of people began to stream slowly into the hall and past the coffin. For the next two days, mourners continued to pack the hall. It was estimated that, by the time the doors were closed for the last time late on Friday evening before the funeral the following day, at least 200,000 folk from all walks of life and all ranks and classes had visited to pay homage to the dead statesman. A standard bearer, drummer and trumpeter from the 2nd Life Guards led the procession to the Abbey, where a congregation of 2,500 mourners awaited its arrival. The picture below shows the Lord Chancellor leading the mace bearer, bishops and chaplains of the House of Lords on their way to Westminster Abbey. The actual Guard of Honour was made up of boys from Eton, Gladstone's old school.

Lord Salisbury offered the Gladstone family a choice of funeral arrangements. If they wished, the Grand Old Man could be buried with all the pomp and pageantry the state could muster, but this would take time to arrange. The alternative was a more simple, immediate ceremony, and the family chose the latter. Accordingly, on 25 May, the former Prime Minister was laid in a simple wooden coffin made by the local carpenter and carried by special train from his home at Hawarden to London. His body lay in solemn state in Westminster Hall, where thousands of people filed slowly past by day and night to pay their last respects.

'Ashes to ashes'

The funeral took place the following Saturday morning in Westminster Abbey. It was attended by everyone who mattered, from the Prince of Wales downwards. The crowds thronged Parliament Square to witness the funeral procession to the Abbey. According to the *New York Times*, apart from the tolling of the funeral bells, the only sound to break the silence as the cortege passed was that of 'a solitary husky voice, which shouted "God give ye rest, old man".' Salisbury, Balfour, Lord Kimberley, William Harcourt, the Dukes of York and Rutland, Lord Rendel, George Armitstead and the Prince of Wales himself were pall-bearers.

The Archbishop of Canterbury, Bishop of London and Dean of Westminster presided over the service, which was short but impressive. Afterwards, while Handel's 'Dead March' was played on the organ, Gladstone's widow knelt in prayer by the grave, until her sons gently helped her to a chair set ready for her by the graveside. One by one, led by the Prince of Wales, the pall-bearers went to her and stooped to kiss her hand. She spoke a few brief words to each of them; Salisbury, she later recalled, had been too deeply moved to say anything.

Among all the grieving, there was one person who remained unmoved. The Queen could not be persuaded to officially express her regret at Gladstone's death. Perhaps it would have been hypocritical if she had – she had never hidden her dislike of the man and he was, after all, almost 90 years old. She complained to Salisbury about 'the extraordinary fuss' and telegraphed the Prince of Wales, asking what advice he had taken and what precedent he had followed before offering to be a pall-bearer. The Prince, who had always liked and respected Gladstone, replied that he had sought no advice and knew of no precedent.

Gladstone's funeral was headline news. Reporting to the Queen on the occasion, Salisbury commented on the great crowds that gathered outside the Abbey to witness the event. He added that 'the effect was made almost ridiculous by the rows of cameras which lined the pavement and the roofs'. There were even some primitive newsreel film cameras on hand recording the scene.

AVENGING GORDON

Far away in Egypt, there were fewer reporters on hand as General Sir Herbert Kitchener embarked on the last stages of his mission to re-capture Sudan and Khartoum from the Dervishes. Kitchener distrusted and disliked most newspapermen on principle. There were 26 war correspondents accompanying his forces as they slowly advanced southwards up the River Nile. Each of them was allowed to cable home despatches of not more than 200 words a day. There were no official briefings – nor were they offered any help or guidance. In fact, they were treated with the barest courtesy.

Kitchener had been pressing for the campaign of re-conquest in Sudan ever since he had been appointed sirdar (commander in chief) of the Anglo-Egyptian army in 1892. He and Sir Evelyn Baring, the imperial proconsul and ruler of Egypt in all but name, argued that reasserting British control of the upper waters of the Nile was essential for Egyptian security. If things were left as they were, they warned, there was every danger that France or some other rival European power might step into the breach.

In 1896 the government finally gave Kitchener and Baring the go-ahead. Initially Kitchener was authorised only to advance as far as Dongola, a strategically important town just above the Nile's Third Cataract, some 640 miles north of the Sudanese capital. He had 8,200 British and 17,600 Egyptian and Sudanese troops under his command. He took the town that June, then halted.

Salisbury needed time to gather together the means to pay for a renewed advance. It had been hoped, somewhat optimistically, that other great powers would contribute to the cost of Kitchener's expedition by allowing the *Caisse de la Dette Publique*, the international body that virtually controlled the Egyptian economy, to release the funds. In the event, the French and Russians vetoed the suggestion. Salisbury told the Queen that 'the question of going forward to

Khartoum is purely a question of money. If it is to be done, it must be done with English funds.' Once the funds were available, Kitchener – who had put the delay to good use, securing his communications by building a rail link across the desert – was cleared to continue the advance.

On to Omdurman

With the great advance starting, a pushy young cavalry lieutenant was soon on his way from London to join the Anglo-Egyptian forces. His name was Winston Churchill. Kitchener had done his best to veto the move, but Churchill and Lady Randolph, his redoubtable mother, went over his head. They used their enormous social and political influence to get the Prime Minister and the War Office to allow Winston to take part in the campaign. Eventually, Sir Evelyn Wood, the Adjutant-General, agreed to despatch him to serve as a supernumerary lieutenant with the 21st Lancers. 'It is understood,' Churchill's orders ran, 'that you will proceed at your own expense and that in the event of your being killed or wounded in the impending operations or for any other reason, no charge of any kind will fall on British Army funds.'

Churchill was unperturbed. As Kitchener had suspected, he intended to combine his military duties with those of war correspondent. He had a commission from the *Morning Post*, whose editor had agreed to pay the princely sum of £15 for every article that the newspaper published. With his orders in his pocket, Churchill set off speedily for Cairo, where he joined his new regiment as it began the arduous 1,400-mile journey up the Nile. It took them nearly three weeks to reach the front. They travelled by train and steamship, before marching the final 200 miles through the blistering desert heat in full battle array. A few hours after they reached their final camp, they got their first sight of the enemy.

'The nominal suzerain of Egypt is the Sultan, its real suzerain is Lord Cromer [Sir Evelyn Baring]. Its nominal governor is the Khedive, its real governor is Thomas Cook'

George Steevens, war correspondent

Slaughter of the Dervishes

While the gunboats and some of the howitzers were sent on upriver to pound the defences of Omdurman and shell the Mahdi's tomb, Kitchener ordered the bulk of his forces to draw up in a horseshoe formation, with its back to the Nile. The resulting semicircle stretched for some 4,000 yards, with each frontline battalion deploying six companies in the firing line with two in reserve. They took shelter for the night behind what in Arabic is called a *zariba*, a tall barricade of thorn bushes, erected for protection from sudden enemy attack.

Shortly after daybreak on 2 September, 1898, the Battle of Omdurman commenced with what one observer described as an 'awful noise' – it was the sound of the advancing Dervish army. The Dervishes soon came into sight, as Drill Sergeant Morgan of the Grenadier Guards later recorded: '... an enormous host with spears and shields had gathered in the early sun ... The sights and sounds seemed to create a queer feeling among the young chaps, but they immediately stiffened up and remembered they were Britons!'

NILE GRANDEUR
Far from the fighting, two intrepid ladies scale the giant statues that dominate the facade of the temple built at Abu Simbel by the ancient Egyptian pharaoh, Rameses II. Their guide, with a fellow tourist, can be seen below shielding their eyes from the sun. Another temple nearby was built to honour Nefertari, Rameses' favourite wife. Located near Aswan, the temples became required visiting for the growing number of well-to-do British tourists. In 1890 Thomas Cook, the leading travel agent of the day, had no fewer than 15 steamers operating as floating hotels on the Nile. The company also built a luxury hotel in Luxor, with superb views across the river to the ruins of ancient Thebes. It was the first hotel constructed by Cook anywhere in the world. There was no doubting Cook's domination of the Egyptian tourist trade.

Lieutenant Ronald Meiklejohn of the Royal Warwickshire Regiment was another eyewitness present who recorded the sight: 'All along the crests of the high ground to our right,' he wrote, 'a solid black multitude of men began to appear. Soon after, another mass appeared over Signal Hill ridge ...' The Dervishes, Meiklejohn noted, 'were moving forward fairly quickly. Then they suddenly slowed down, made a really orderly "right wheel" and deployed into one huge and nearly uninterrupted line and came straight at us. Earle, our Adjutant, came galloping up and shouted "Get into your places please, Gentlemen, the show is starting," and we took up our stations.'

Much to Kitchener's amazement, the Dervishes had launched a full frontal assault on his well-equipped army, secure in a strong defensive position. As the Dervish line closed in, the Anglo-Egyptian artillery started to shell them. Then the infantry opened up with blistering and continuous rifle volleys, supported by rapid machine-gun fire, that cut the well-ordered Dervish ranks to shreds.

George Steevens, the most celebrated war correspondent of the day, wrote a vivid account of the carnage. 'They came very fast and very straight; and then presently they came no further. With a crash the bullets leapt out of the British rifles. It began with the Guards and Warwicks – section volleys at 200 yards – and then, as the Dervishes edged rightward, it ran along to the Highlanders, the Lincolns and to Maxwell's Brigade. The British stood up in double rank behind their *zariba*; the Sudanese lay down in their shelter-trench. Both poured out death as fast as they could load and press trigger. Shrapnel whistled and Maxims grunted savagely.'

The Lancers charge

Serious firing started at 7.00 in the morning; just an hour later, Steevens noted, 'the plain was still again'. Another half hour went by and then a shrill bugle call signalled to Kitchener's men that the time had come to advance. The Anglo-Egyptian army slowly started to move forward as the surviving Dervishes streamed back towards Omdurman. Determined to put a stop to the retreat, Kitchener ordered the 21st Lancers into action. 'Annoy them as much as possible on their flank', he ordered, 'and head them off if possible from Omdurman.'

Lieutenant-Colonel Rowland Martin, the Lancers' commanding officer, was eager to see action, for the 21st Lancers had the dubious honour of being the only regiment in the entire British army without any battle honours to its credit. It was quipped that its motto was 'thou shalt not kill'. So when he and his men saw what appeared to be a small band of Dervish cavalry plus a few foot soldiers caught in the open, he gave the order to charge.

It was a trap. Behind the Dervishes that the Lancers could see, a shrewd Dervish commander had concealed some 2,000 men in a small rocky depression. By the time the British realised what they were charging into, it was impossible for them to stop. According to Bennet Burleigh, the war correspondent of the *Daily Telegraph*, what followed was 'a moment or two of wild work, thrusting of steel, lance and sword and rapid revolver shooting' before the Lancers managed to fight their way out of the depression and rally some 200 yards away.

The action was short – Churchill, who was right in the thick of it, estimated that it lasted no longer than two minutes. Yet it was costly: 26 men, almost a quarter of those taking part, were wounded and nine men were killed. Three of the survivors were awarded the Victoria Cross for gallantry. After the event,

VENGEANCE OF THE VICTOR
The Mahdi's tomb at Omdurman shows the damage inflicted on it by shellfire from British gunboats stationed on the River Nile during the build-up to the battle there on 2 September, 1898. This illustration of

the shell-damaged tomb was based on a photograph taken at the time by Captain E A Stanton. The Mahdi had died in June 1885, less than six months after defeating Gordon; it was the Khalifa, his successor, whom Kitchener defeated. After the battle, the tomb was quickly looted and the victorious Kitchener ordered its destruction. The Mahdi's remains were disinterred and, with the exception of his 'unusually large and shapely' skull, were unceremoniously thrown into the Nile. There was talk of mounting the skull in silver or gold and turning it into an inkstand or a drinking cup, but the Queen, shocked by the desecration, ordered Lord Salisbury to ensure that it was given a decent burial. The tomb itself was later restored.

'It occurred to me that, if the action was to begin in an hour, it would be prudent to have some lunch … Standing at a table spread in the wilderness, we ate a substantial meal. It was like a race lunch before the big event.'

W S Churchill, *The River War*, 1899

opinions differed as to whether the charge had been wise. Lieutenant-General Francis Grenfell, commanding officer in Egypt, wrote that, 'despite the heavy losses in killed and wounded', the action 'was worthy of the best traditions of the British cavalry'. On the other hand, Lieutenant Meiklejohn recorded, 'We hear that the charge was a great error and K is furious'.

There was one more surprise in store for Kitchener. As his infantry began its advance on Omdurman, its right flank was left open to counter-attack. Luckily, Colonel Hector Macdonald, commander of the 1st Sudanese Brigade, saw the danger and acted quickly to repel a Dervish attack. The survivors melted away into the desert. After the battle Kitchener commented contentedly to his staff: 'I think we've given them a good dusting, gentlemen.' Anglo-Egyptian losses were 51 dead and 382 wounded. Between 10,000 and 11,000 Dervishes were killed, another 16,000 wounded and 5,000 more taken prisoner. It was little wonder that a grateful British government rewarded Kitchener with a peerage, the Order of the Bath and a grant of £30,000.

BATTLE CASUALTIES
A group of British officers, wounded in the Battle of Omdurman, convalesce outside the military hospital in Abadia. The victory, wrote the young Winston Churchill, was 'the most signal triumph ever gained by the arms of science over barbarians'.

THE CONQUERING HEROES
Lieutenant de Montmorency (seated centre) and other survivors of the cavalry charge at Omdurman pose for the camera (top). De Montmorency valiantly tried to rescue the body of a fallen fellow officer after the charge. He was one of three officers of the 21st Lancers to be awarded the Victoria Cross for their gallant conduct during the battle, which won universal praise, even from those who deemed the charge itself unwise. In his book *With Kitchener to Khartoum*, war correspondent George Steevens wrote that the gallantry displayed by the young de Montmorency was just one of the 'many deeds of self-abandoning heroism of which tale the half will not be told'. African auxiliaries, too, served bravely for Britain in the Anglo-Egyptian army; here (centre) Kitchener is greeted by a band of hill tribesmen warriors at Roseine.

When Kitchener eventually returned home, at the end of October 1898, he received a tumultuous reception, starting with the cheering crowds that greeted his arrival at Dover (bottom; Kitchener is in the centre, wearing a bowler hat). He was raised to the peerage, awarded a grant of £30,000 and voted the thanks of Parliament for his efforts. Lord Salisbury told the House of Lords that 'the honour that has been paid to him throughout the length and breadth of the land is a sufficient proof that the people of this country entirely associate themselves with the action of Her Majesty in conferring that honour on him.' Only a few Radical MPs and Irish Nationalists disagreed, and they came in for heavy criticism. Frederick Carne Rasch, the Conservative MP for Southeast Essex, castigated the objectors as 'people who always find Englishmen in the wrong all over the world, and foreigners in the right. They have friends in every country in which the nation has enemies.'

KHARTOUM IN RUINS
Anglo-Egyptian troops survey the ruins of Khartoum after their triumphal entry into the city following victory at Omdurman. Kitchener's first act was to order a memorial service to commemorate General Gordon's last stand. It was held in front of the ruins of the palace where Gordon had met his death. The Royal Engineers were then ordered to superintend the rebuilding of the city, following sketch plans drawn up by Kitchener himself.

When the news of Kitchener's triumph reached home, extraordinary mass celebrations broke out. As Salisbury noted, it was as if what he termed 'the intoxication of the Jubilee' had returned as the crowds took to the streets. The victory, he said, was 'a wonderful display of tenacity and foresight on the part of Kitchener and Cromer' (as Sir Evelyn Baring was known after being made a peer, Lord Cromer). But the three men now faced what seemed to be, for a time, an even more formidable challenge.

The Fashoda incident

The French had always regretted their decision not to take part in the occupation of Egypt when Gladstone had offered them the chance to do so. Now, they decided to take control of the Nile's headwaters. In June 1896, Commandant Jean-Baptiste Marchand, a seasoned French veteran of several West African campaigns, left the coast and started out eastwards. His orders were to proceed to the Bahr al-Ghazal region of the Upper Sudan, some 2,000 miles away, and take control of Fashoda, an abandoned fort on the west bank of the White Nile. After an epic march – in itself a remarkable feat of courage and endurance – Marchand eventually reached his goal on 10 July, 1898, and raised the tricolour.

Following secret orders from Salisbury, Kitchener reacted immediately, as soon as he had won his battle against the Dervishes. Backed by a vastly superior force, he raced up the Nile to Fashoda, arriving there on 18 September. The scene was set for a major confrontation between the two great powers. In Paris, nationalist newspapers, such as *Le Gaulois*, openly called for war. Back home in Britain, even the Liberal Opposition supported Salisbury in his refusal to concede anything to meet French demands. Lord Rosebery declared that no British government that gave way over Fashoda would last a week.

It was a question of who would back down first. Patiently, Salisbury negotiated his way through the crisis, though he did take the precaution of mobilising the Mediterranean fleet. Eventually, the French government gave in, telling the British premier that, 'in view of the precarious situation and the state of health of Marchand and his companions', it had ordered him to withdraw.

Salisbury broke the news at a banquet in Kitchener's honour held at the Mansion House in the City of London on 4 November. As soon as it reached the ears of the thousands who had lined the streets to greet Kitchener, they broke into spontaneous cheering. 'It keeps the French entirely out of the Nile Valley', a contented premier later told the Queen. Britain had won a bloodless victory and the danger of full-scale war had been averted.

STRIKES AND LOCK-OUTS

SHOWDOWN AT FASHODA
General Kitchener and Commandant Jean-Baptiste Marchand, leader of a tiny French expedition, in conference at Fashoda, a strategically important fort on the banks of the White Nile. Though the two men got on well, drinking whisky and champagne together and congratulating each other on their respective achievements, the so-called Fashoda incident brought Britain and France within a hair's breadth of war. Eventually, faced with determined British diplomatic pressure, the French gave way and the gallant Marchand was ordered to withdraw.

While Kitchener's army was advancing up the Nile towards its date with destiny at Omdurman, the South Wales coal fields were at a standstill. The miners there were in a life-or-death struggle with colliery owners to maintain a living wage. They were paid on a sliding scale for the amount of coal produced, depending on how much it brought on the open market. When prices fell, the miners' wages fell. What the miners wanted was a fixed minimum price per ton and to have the sliding scale removed from the wage calculation.

Attempts to negotiate a settlement came to nothing. After a bitter six-month lock-out, the dispute ended with the miners forced to capitulate to the owners' terms and return to work. Over 100,000 of them subsequently joined the newly formed South Wales Miners' Federation.

The previous year, a similar lock-out had paralysed the engineering industry for several months. It also ended with victory for the employers. During the Jubilee celebrations Sir Michael Hicks Beach, the Chancellor of the Exchequer, had predicted that generations would pass before 'the British people reach again so high a level of widely diffused comforts, of financial ease both public and private, of social and political contentment, of class union, of world power, and of superiority to foreign rivalry and competition'. As far as many ordinary working-class folk were concerned, his words now rang hollow indeed.

CITIES OF SMOKE AND STEEL

A man and his workhorse cross a river in Leeds on a hand-pulled ferry, as the chimneys of the Coghlan Steel Works behind them belch clouds of smoke into the sky. The history of steel-making in the region stretched back into the mid-18th century, but it was Leeds's neighbouring Yorkshire city of Sheffield that built a reputation as the capital of steel, largely thanks to Thomas Bessemer. Following the invention of the Bessemer Converter, to transform pig iron into quality steel, Bessemer had moved his factory to Sheffield in 1858.

On the surface, in Sheffield and around the country, things looked prosperous enough, but by the 1890s Britain was fast being caught and even overtaken by its industrial rivals. While the British steel industry barely doubled its output between 1880 and 1914, German steel production multiplied nearly ten times. Some people tried to shake the nation out of its apparent complacency. The *Daily Express* ran a series of articles entitled 'Wake Up England' and the *Daily Mail* followed suit with a series on 'American Invaders'. Yet most industrialists seemed content to carry on in the same old ways. When one Yorkshire ironmaster was presented with a copy of the *Principles of Scientific Management* by its American author, his reply was to send back a work of his own. It was an edition of *Horace's Odes,* in the original Latin, of course.

IN THE DOCKS

A group of dock workers (left) pose for a group photograph outside the offices of one of the London dock employers. Less formally, officials watch the camera while a ship is unloaded (below). The incoming cargo at West India Dock awaits transport through customs to the warehouses (right). At the end of the previous decade, low pay and poor conditions – most dockers were casual labourers, hired and fired as and when work was available – had led to the Great London Dock Strike. Against all odds, the dockers won, but initial attempts to establish similar conditions elsewhere had mixed results. A strike at Southampton in 1890 was called off after a few days. But on the whole, the docks avoided the worst industrial strife of the decade and carried on the work of shipping goods to and from the Empire and the Mother Country.

There were government attempts to help. Lord Salisbury's administration tried, unsuccessfully, to revitalise the countryside by passing measures to help farmers out of the agricultural recession. Thanks to Joseph Chamberlain, who had not totally forgotten his Radical origins, the Workmen's Compensation Act was passed. This established that injured workmen – or, rather, certain defined classes of workmen – had the right to seek compensation from government funds for injury sustained at work. But other obvious reforms, such as Old Age Pensions, which Chamberlain had long been advocating, were stillborn.

For their part, working people were slowly starting to turn away from the old political allegiances towards a new one. In 1899, albeit narrowly, the Trades Union Congress – itself now gaining in strength – voted for the establishment of an autonomous Labour Party. Early the following year, the Labour Representation Committee was formed.

THE HIGH STREET

During the 1890s, national chains of shops emerged in Britain, with the ability to undercut their more traditional rivals. In the food trade, for instance, Lipton's had started off modestly in Glasgow with a single shop, but by 1898 it had 250 branches around the country. Department stores, offering a huge variety of goods under one roof, were also changing the way people shopped. In 1896 Lady Mary Jeune noted: 'We go to purchase something we want; but when we get to our shop there are so many more things that we never thought of …'. But small shops, especially food shops, continued to hold their own on local high streets.

ATTRACTIVE DISPLAY
The bakery window in Scot Lane, Doncaster, displays cakes, buns and biscuits for every occasion. Nuttalls' Rum and Butter Drops, at 1 penny for 3 ounces, and Fry's chocolate bars were branded items that were also sure sellers. The 'delicious ices in all flavours' were probably made on the premises, like the cakes. Truly local tradesmen, like this butcher in Doncaster (far left), let their wares speak for themselves. Even as late as the 1890s, it was still the custom for such tradesmen to call on customers to collect their orders, which were then delivered to the door.

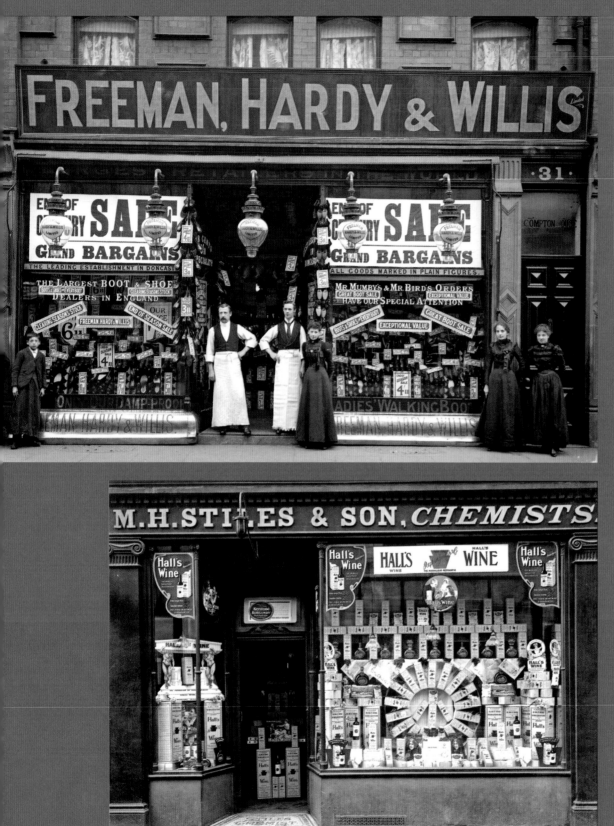

THE ART OF SELLING

A Doncaster boot repair shop (right) has an eye-catching window display. With the arrival of rubber, boot and shoe-making had been industrialised. Instead of being made to order for customers who were personally measured, boots and shoes were mass-produced in standard sizes. By 1896, C and J Clarke, the country's largest shoe-maker, offered 225 varieties of boots, 353 of shoes and 144 of slippers.

Freeman, Hardy & Willis (top left) sold 'shoes for all the family' on a massive scale. From establishing a first shop in 1875, the company grew and grew; by the turn of the century, there was an FH&W branch in practically every town. Small boot-makers did not give up without a fight. This advert for Salisbury boots (above) was produced by Moore Bros in Salisbury. They claimed to sell the 'very finest goods at much below West-End prices'.

Local chemists (left) were facing considerable competition from bigger rivals, such as Boots, which had grown from humble begins as a herbalist's shop into a nationwide chain. The Hall's Wine prominently advertised in this chemist's window was a well-known health drink – or, as the Hall's company preferred to put it, 'the supreme tonic restorative'.

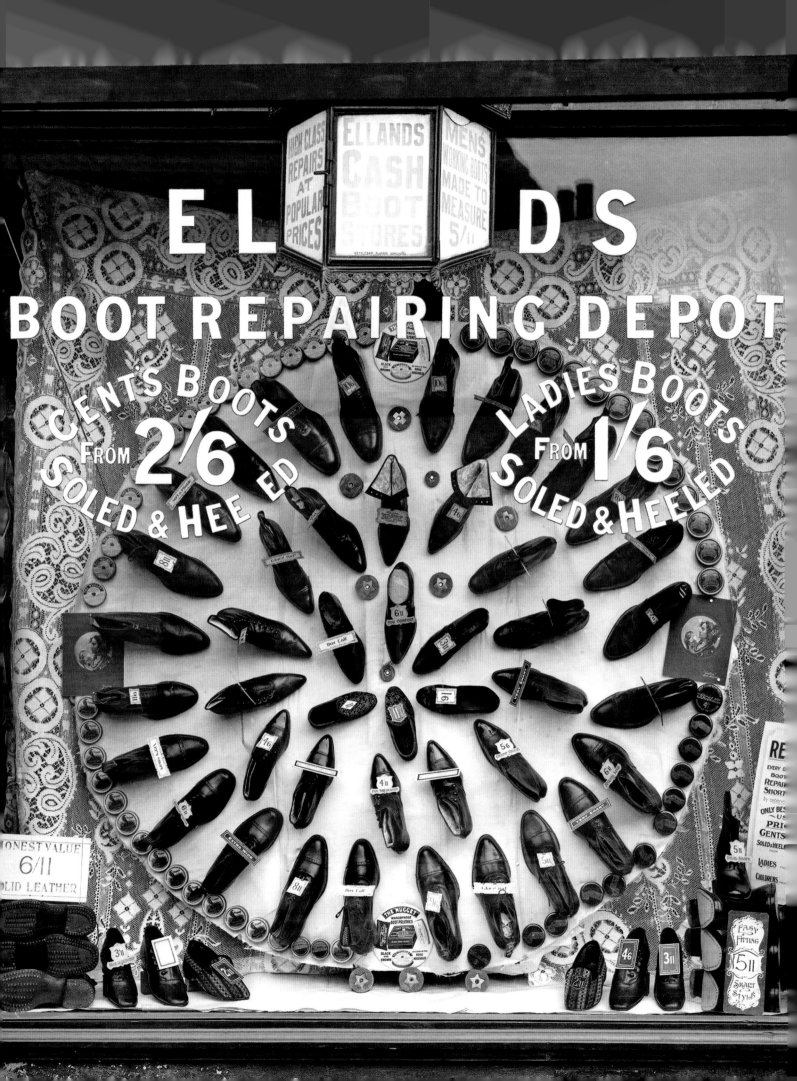

STREET MARKETS

Markets were part and parcel of daily life in the 1890s, even though their numbers were starting to dwindle as shops gained ground. Most market traders remained small, local businessmen, but there was one notable exception. In 1884 Michael Marks, a Russian-born Polish refugee, set up a stall at Kirkgate Market in Leeds. His boast was that he sold everything for no more than a penny. Ten years later, he set up his first shop, in Manchester, and went into partnership with Tom Spencer. From these humble beginnings, the retail giant Marks & Spencer would grow.

FRIENDLY GIANT

London's main fruit, vegetable and flower market was centrally located in Covent Garden. The author of *Cruchley's London* noted that of all the markets it was 'the most agreeable in the Metropolis'. Work here started early. Dr Andrew Wynter, a keen observer of London, wrote in the *Quarterly Review* how 'as early as two o'clock in the morning, a person looking down the dip of Piccadilly will perceive the first influx of the daily supply of vegetables and fruit'.

HUSTLE AND BUSTLE

The New Cut, south of the Thames in Lambeth, was one long market of over 200 shops and up to 300 stalls. According to *Daily News* journalist Joseph Parkinson, stalls here were still open at midnight, selling 'huge lumps of fine celery at a penny a lot, fried and cured fish at 1d and 2d, tea and sugar at minimum prices … and quack pills for "wind" and "worms".' It was, noted another observer, true 'Mercantile Pandemonium'.

FRESH FROM THE SEA
Passers-by haggle with local fishermen at the celebrated fish market on Brighton beach. The catch was landed directly onto the beach, fresh from the boat The Victorians loved fish provided that it was fresh, which could be a challenge in these days before home refrigeration. For special occasions, blocks of ice could be purchased, but normally the best that could be managed was to store the fish in a cool cellar or a pantry on a north-facing wall. The best bet was to eat fish on the day it was purchased. There was a wealth of fish to choose from, but for the thrifty, a cod's head was recommended as a particularly good buy, as 'almost every part is considered good eating except the eyes'.

FISH IN THE CITY
Market porters at London's Billingsgate, 'a free and open market for the landing and bringing in of all sorts of fish', according to the statute that originally established the market in the 17th century. Dr Andrew Wynter described a visit to Billingsgate in late Victorian times: 'The noisy scene … between the hours of five and seven in the morning, is one of the wonders of the metropolis … Nearly one-half of the fish supply of London is hurried in the dead of night across the length and breadth of the land to Billingsgate, where it may be seen lying on the marble slabs of the fishmongers.' The volume of trade was staggering. In a single year it was estimated that some 400,000 cod were sold, 2.47 million haddock, 23.62 million mackerel and 97.5 million sole. Salmon was also popular: vast quantities were shipped down from Aberdeen by special train. Among shellfish, oysters were a particular favourite, with an estimated 500 million sold a year, prompting wit and playwright W S Gilbert to wonder 'what on earth becomes of the shells?'

FROM DISASTER TO VICTORY
General Sir Redvers Buller (left) lost his military reputation in South Africa, when the forces he commanded were trounced by the Boers in three successive battles in December 1899. 'Black Week', as it quickly became known, led to Lord Roberts (right) being sent out to replace Buller as commander in chief, with Lord Kitchener as his chief of staff. What tipped the scales against Buller retaining his post was not so much his defeat at Colenso – where Roberts' only son was killed in the battle – but a telegram he sent to Lord Lansdowne, Britain's Secretary of State at War, stating that his forces were not strong enough to relieve besieged Ladysmith. He ought, he said, 'to let Ladysmith go, and occupy good positions for the defence of Natal'. The government were not prepared to put up with such defeatism.

Roberts was eager for the fray. Ever since his successes in Afghanistan, he had been a national hero; Kipling had paid him affectionate tribute in one of his best-known poems, simply entitled 'Bobs'. Not for nothing was he known as 'the pocket Napoleon'. Scorning Buller's dilatory approach – on his arrival in South Africa, he commented scornfully that the war was being waged 'like a game of polo, with intervals for afternoon tea' – he and Kitchener reorganised the British forces and set off on a swift flanking march. Piet Cronje, the leading Boer commander, was defeated in a full-scale battle and forced to surrender on 27 February, 1900. The very next day, Buller, still in local command in Natal, finally fought his way through to Ladysmith and lifted the siege. The war was far from over, but the tide had surely been turned.

obdurate, bolstered by a public promise of support from his fellow-Boers in the Orange Free State. Finally, on 29 September, 1899, Salisbury and his Cabinet agreed to send the Boers an ultimatum. It was on its way to South Africa by the extraordinarily slow process of mail steamer when Milner was handed an ultimatum from the Boers. It stated bluntly that, if 'the troops on the borders of this republic [the Transvaal]' were not 'instantly withdrawn' and all British reinforcements 'removed', the Boers would go to war.

Salisbury's response was instant and predictable. He instructed Milner to reply that 'the conditions demanded by the South African Republic are such as HMG deems it impossible to discuss'. The Boers attacked in Natal the following day.

'Black Week'

At home, people expected that the war would be short. It would be over, they said, in a matter of weeks. Moberly Bell, the manager of *The Times*, confidently predicted that by 'about the 15 December, we shall have here in South Africa a nice little Army and all the materials for a respectable war save the enemy'. Few in Britain foresaw that the two tiny Boer republics, with a combined white population less than that of London, would manage to hold the mighty British Empire at bay for over two-and-a-half years. Nor did anyone dream that it would take an army of some 400,000 troops to subdue them.

The war began badly for the British – and then things went from bad to worse. By the end of October, the Boers had totally outmanoeuvred General Sir George White, commander of the Natal Field Force. He and his men were bottled up in Ladysmith, which was promptly besieged. So, too, was the diamond town of Kimberley, on the northernmost border of Cape Province. Mafeking, from which Jameson and his men had set off on their notorious raid three years earlier, was the third town to be surrounded. Cecil Rhodes was trapped in Kimberley, while in Mafeking Robert Baden-Powell dug in resolutely to wait until help arrived. It was to be a long time in coming.

It did not help that, initially at least, the Boers could actually put more men into the field than the British. Furthermore, they were better armed with modern Mauser rifles and the latest Krupp and Creusot artillery. However, it soon looked as though the British troops' greatest enemy was their own High Command. Sir Redvers Buller, who would be nicknamed 'Sir Reverse' by his critics, committed blunder after blunder.

Buller arrived in South Africa on 31 October, 1899. Immediately, he was pressurised by a panic-stricken Sir Alfred Milner into taking quick and decisive action. Fatefully, Buller decided to split his army corps into three. He ordered Lord Methuen, in command of 20,000 men of the 1st Division, to advance to relieve

BOERS IN THE FIELD
Boer artillerymen firing a Creusot 'Long Tom' siege gun outside Mafeking in 1899 (below). The Boers were well equipped and they were also excellent soldiers. They were more than a match for the British regulars – and certainly for the British commanders in charge at the start of the war. When Buller attacked Boer positions at Colenso, his forces were quickly driven back across the Tugela River, despite having a three-to-one numerical advantage. It was not until Lord Roberts doubled the number of mounted infantry that the British could match the mobility of adversaries like these mounted Boer scouts (right).

FIGHTING FORCE
Boer troops man a trench outside Mafeking
at the start of the war. Almost eight
thousand Boers were involved in the siege,
out of 35,000 men mobilised at the start of
the war. Baden-Powell and the Mafeking
garrison held on grimly, not only tying down
this large fighting force, but also driving the
Boers back when a last-ditch attempt to
storm the town was launched. Inside
Mafeking conditions had grown steadily
worse, but morale remained high. Lady
Sarah Wilson recorded how 'breakfast
consists of horse sausages; lunch, minced
mule and curried locusts.'

BOERS IN BATTLE
BURGHERS SLAAGS.

BREAKING THE NEWS
A group of war correspondents (top right)
bound for South Africa; Winston Churchill is
second from left in the middle row.
Practically every major newspaper had
correspondents on the spot. As well as
cabling back news, many correspondents
now had the latest Pocket and Bullet Kodak
cameras, which meant that, for the first
time, action photographs could be sent
back from the theatre of war. There were
motion pictures, too, mostly shot by
W K L Dickson, a bioscope pioneer.

Churchill was soon captured during a
Boer attack on an armoured reconnaissance
train. He was held in a prison camp in
Pretoria with other British prisoners of war
(right), but decided to attempt an escape
when he was informed that there was little
chance of him being released. He climbed
the prison wall at night while the sentries'
backs were turned, then made his way
through the town to the Delagoa Bay
railway line and jumped a moving goods
train. He got out just before dawn and
spent the day hiding in a wood, with 'a large
vulture' for company. It took him five days,
walking by night and hiding by day, to reach
Middleburg, where he managed to board
another goods train heading directly to
Delagoa, in neutral Portuguese territory. For
most of the time, he lived on chocolate –
'not a satisfying food,' he later commented.

Kimberley, where Cecil Rhodes was threatening to surrender the town to the Boers
unless something was done to rescue him. Lieutenant-General Sir William Gatacre
was ordered to secure the Northern Cape and relieve Baden-Powell in Mafeking.
Buller himself would advance to lift the siege of Ladysmith.

On paper, it all looked practical enough, but the plan soon went horribly
wrong. On 11 December, Methuen walked into a trap set by the Boers at
Magersfontein. He was soundly beaten when he launched a thoroughly ill-judged
attack on their positions after a botched night march. The previous day, Gatacre
had come to grief at Stormberg Junction. It was now all down to Buller, but on
15 December he, too, suffered a major defeat. After crossing the Tugela River, his
troops met with disaster at Colenso. In a futile battle, which was all over in a
couple of hours, Buller was completely out-thought by Louis Botha, his Boer
opposite number. The British lost 145 men killed, 762 wounded and 220 captured
or missing. The Boers lost just 8 men killed and 50 wounded.

Three major defeats in one week – it was christened 'Black Week' by the press
back at home. The nation was stunned. When Buller signalled to General White,
still holding on in Ladysmith, that he should surrender to the Boers, it was clear
that he had completely lost his nerve and would need to be replaced. The
government promptly sacked him, appointing in his place the 67-year-old Lord
Roberts as the new commander in chief, with Kitchener as chief of staff. This was
a war the British were determined to win.

LOOKING TO THE FUTURE

The year 1899 drew to a close in a wave of patriotic fervour. Few in Britain doubted that Roberts and Kitchener would eventually lead the nation to victory in South Africa. Yet those who looked beyond the headlines wondered what the new century would have in store for them and their country.

The times were changing – and changing fast. Over the course of the decade, inventions had come thick and fast: the typewriter, the zip fastener, the vacuum cleaner, X-rays, the motion picture camera and projector, the escalator, the diesel

INTO THE ETHER
The 26-year-old Guglielmo Marconi (left) operating one of his first wireless transmitters. Marconi began his experiments in 1895 in the fields of his father's estate outside Bologna, before moving to London to continue his work. The initial breakthrough came in November 1897, when he erected his first transmitting mast at the Needles, on the Isle of Wight. By the New Year, he was transmitting clear signals across to the mainland. That summer, his work received the royal accolade when he was asked to set up wireless communication between Osborne House, Queen Victoria's summer home on the island, and the royal yacht in Cowes Bay. Concerned about the Prince of Wales's injured knee, the Queen wanted to be kept informed of his progress. No fewer than 150 messages were transmitted successfully.

As time went by, Marconi sent wireless signals over longer and longer distances. In 1899 he sent the first wireless messages across the English Channel from Wimereux on the north coast of France to England. Two years later, 'the wonderful wizard of wireless telegraphy,' as he was dubbed by the *Halifax Herald* in Canada, sent the first signals across the Atlantic from this transmitting station at Poldhu in Cornwall (right) to St John's in Newfoundland. The signals travelled a distance well in excess of 2,000 miles.

'Wireless telegraphy is a possibility anywhere, and it will, I think, soon be a reality in many places.'

Guglielmo Marconi, 1898

engine – these were just a few of the innovations to emerge around the world. Other new technologies were establishing their place. Motor cars were starting to become commonplace, rather than rarities. Telephone communication was expanding as exchanges came on stream.

In March 1899, a 26-year-old Italian inventor called Guglielmo Marconi sent the first wireless signal across the English Channel. The previous year – the year in which H G Wells' *The War of the Worlds* became a best-seller – Germany had signalled its intention of creating a great High Seas Fleet big enough to challenge Britain's traditional naval supremacy. The unanswered question was whether the times were changing for the better.

INDEX

PICTURE ACKNOWLEDGEMENTS

Abbreviations: t = top; m = middle; b = bottom; r = right; c = centre; l = left

All images in this book are courtesy of Getty Images, including the following which have additional attributions:
16, 28, 35b, 36, 39b, 53, 62, 64, 69t, 73, 103, 104, 106, 120b, 122b, 136, 140-1, 142tl, 142b, 143: Popperfoto
17, 25, 50t, 149r: Sean Sexton
23b, 38, 70b, 89, 116t, 142tr, 148, 149l, 155b: Time & Life Pictures
35t: Bridgeman Art Library
44, 121, 129, 135: Roger Viollet
54: Robert Welch
55: Transcendental Graphics
156: Museum of the City of New York

LOOKING BACK AT BRITAIN
VICTORIA'S FINAL DECADE – 1890s
is published by The Reader's Digest Association Ltd, London, in association with Getty Images and Endeavour London Ltd.

Copyright © 2009 The Reader's Digest Association Ltd

The Reader's Digest Association Ltd
11 Westferry Circus
Canary Wharf
London E14 4HE
www.readersdigest.co.uk

Endeavour London Ltd
21–31 Woodfield Road
London W9 2BA
info@endeavourlondon.com

Written by
Jeremy Harwood

For Endeavour
Publisher: Charles Merullo
Designer: Tea Aganovic
Picture editors: Jennifer Jeffrey, Franziska Payer Crockett
Production: Mary Osborne

For Reader's Digest
Project editor: Christine Noble
Art editor: Conorde Clarke
Indexer: Marie Lorimer
Proofreader: Ron Pankhurst
Pre-press account manager: Dean Russell
Product production manager: Claudette Bramble
Production controller: Sandra Fuller

Reader's Digest General Books
Editorial director: Julian Browne
Art director: Anne-Marie Bulat

Colour origination by Chroma Graphics Ltd, Singapore
Printed and bound in China

We are committed both to the quality of our products and the service we provide to our customers. We value your comments, so please do contact us on 08705 113366 or via our website at
www.readersdigest.co.uk

If you have any comments or suggestions about the content of our books, email us at
gbeditorial@readersdigest.co.uk

CONCEPT CODE: UK 0154/L/S
BOOK CODE: 638-007 UP0000-1
ISBN: 978 0 276 44395 4
ORACLE CODE: 356900007H.00.24